# LAYERS OF LEARNING
## YEAR FOUR • UNIT ELEVEN

# WORLD WAR II
# SYMBOLS & LANDMARKS
# AIR & WATER
# WAR ART

Published by HooDoo Publishing
United States of America
© 2017 Layers of Learning

(Grilled Cheese BTN Font) © Fontdiner - www.fontdiner.com
ISBN #978-1547176267

# Units at a Glance: Topics For All Four Years of the Layers of Learning Program

| 1 | History | Geography | Science | The Arts |
|---|---------|-----------|---------|----------|
| 1 | Mesopotamia | Maps & Globes | Planets | Cave Paintings |
| 2 | Egypt | Map Keys | Stars | Egyptian Art |
| 3 | Europe | Global Grids | Earth & Moon | Crafts |
| 4 | Ancient Greece | Wonders | Satellites | Greek Art |
| 5 | Babylon | Mapping People | Humans in Space | Poetry |
| 6 | The Levant | Physical Earth | Laws of Motion | List Poems |
| 7 | Phoenicians | Oceans | Motion | Moral Stories |
| 8 | Assyrians | Deserts | Fluids | Rhythm |
| 9 | Persians | Arctic | Waves | Melody |
| 10 | Ancient China | Forests | Machines | Chinese Art |
| 11 | Early Japan | Mountains | States of Matter | Line & Shape |
| 12 | Arabia | Rivers & Lakes | Atoms | Color & Value |
| 13 | Ancient India | Grasslands | Elements | Texture & Form |
| 14 | Ancient Africa | Africa | Bonding | African Tales |
| 15 | First North Americans | North America | Salts | Creative Kids |
| 16 | Ancient South America | South America | Plants | South American Art |
| 17 | Celts | Europe | Flowering Plants | Jewelry |
| 18 | Roman Republic | Asia | Trees | Roman Art |
| 19 | Christianity | Australia & Oceania | Simple Plants | Instruments |
| 20 | Roman Empire | You Explore | Fungi | Composing Music |

| 2 | History | Geography | Science | The Arts |
|---|---------|-----------|---------|----------|
| 1 | Byzantines | Turkey | Climate & Seasons | Byzantine Art |
| 2 | Barbarians | Ireland | Forecasting | Illumination |
| 3 | Islam | Arabian Peninsula | Clouds & Precipitation | Creative Kids |
| 4 | Vikings | Norway | Special Effects | Viking Art |
| 5 | Anglo Saxons | Britain | Wild Weather | King Arthur Tales |
| 6 | Charlemagne | France | Cells & DNA | Carolingian Art |
| 7 | Normans | Nigeria | Skeletons | Canterbury Tales |
| 8 | Feudal System | Germany | Muscles, Skin, Cardio | Gothic Art |
| 9 | Crusades | Balkans | Digestive & Senses | Religious Art |
| 10 | Burgundy, Venice, Spain | Switzerland | Nerves | Oil Paints |
| 11 | Wars of the Roses | Russia | Health | Minstrels & Plays |
| 12 | Eastern Europe | Hungary | Metals | Printmaking |
| 13 | African Kingdoms | Mali | Carbon Chemistry | Textiles |
| 14 | Asian Kingdoms | Southeast Asia | Non-metals | Vivid Language |
| 15 | Mongols | Caucasus | Gases | Fun With Poetry |
| 16 | Medieval China & Japan | China | Electricity | Asian Arts |
| 17 | Pacific Peoples | Micronesia | Circuits | Arts of the Islands |
| 18 | American Peoples | Canada | Technology | Indian Legends |
| 19 | The Renaissance | Italy | Magnetism | Renaissance Art I |
| 20 | Explorers | Caribbean Sea | Motors | Renaissance Art II |

| 3 | History | Geography | Science | The Arts |
|---|---------|-----------|---------|----------|
| 1 | Age of Exploration | Argentina & Chile | Classification & Insects | Fairy Tales |
| 2 | The Ottoman Empire | Egypt & Libya | Reptiles & Amphibians | Poetry |
| 3 | Mogul Empire | Pakistan & Afghanistan | Fish | Mogul Arts |
| 4 | Reformation | Angola & Zambia | Birds | Reformation Art |
| 5 | Renaissance England | Tanzania & Kenya | Mammals & Primates | Shakespeare |
| 6 | Thirty Years' War | Spain | Sound | Baroque Music |
| 7 | The Dutch | Netherlands | Light & Optics | Baroque Art I |
| 8 | France | Indonesia | Bending Light | Baroque Art II |
| 9 | The Enlightenment | Korean Peninsula | Color | Art Journaling |
| 10 | Russia & Prussia | Central Asia | History of Science | Watercolors |
| 11 | Conquistadors | Baltic States | Igneous Rocks | Creative Kids |
| 12 | Settlers | Peru & Bolivia | Sedimentary Rocks | Native American Art |
| 13 | 13 Colonies | Central America | Metamorphic Rocks | Settler Sayings |
| 14 | Slave Trade | Brazil | Gems & Minerals | Colonial Art |
| 15 | The South Pacific | Australasia | Fossils | Principles of Art |
| 16 | The British in India | India | Chemical Reactions | Classical Music |
| 17 | The Boston Tea Party | Japan | Reversible Reactions | Folk Music |
| 18 | Founding Fathers | Iran | Compounds & Solutions | Rococo |
| 19 | Declaring Independence | Samoa & Tonga | Oxidation & Reduction | Creative Crafts I |
| 20 | The American Revolution | South Africa | Acids & Bases | Creative Crafts II |

| 4 | History | Geography | Science | The Arts |
|---|---------|-----------|---------|----------|
| 1 | American Government | USA | Heat & Temperature | Patriotic Music |
| 2 | Expanding Nation | Pacific States | Motors & Engines | Tall Tales |
| 3 | Industrial Revolution | U.S. Landscapes | Energy | Romantic Art I |
| 4 | Revolutions | Mountain West States | Energy Sources | Romantic Art II |
| 5 | Africa | U.S. Political Maps | Energy Conversion | Impressionism I |
| 6 | The West | Southwest States | Earth Structure | Impressionism II |
| 7 | Civil War | National Parks | Plate Tectonics | Post Impressionism |
| 8 | World War I | Plains States | Earthquakes | Expressionism |
| 9 | Totalitarianism | U.S. Economics | Volcanoes | Abstract Art |
| 10 | Great Depression | Heartland States | Mountain Building | Kinds of Art |
| 11 | World War II | Symbols & Landmarks | Chemistry of Air & Water | War Art |
| 12 | Modern East Asia | The South | Food Chemistry | Modern Art |
| 13 | India's Independence | People of America | Industry | Pop Art |
| 14 | Israel | Appalachian States | Chemistry of Farming | Modern Music |
| 15 | Cold War | U.S. Territories | Chemistry of Medicine | Free Verse |
| 16 | Vietnam War | Atlantic States | Food Chains | Photography |
| 17 | Latin America | New England States | Animal Groups | Latin American Art |
| 18 | Civil Rights | Home State Study I | Instincts | Theater & Film |
| 19 | Technology | Home State Study II | Habitats | Architecture |
| 20 | Terrorism | America in Review | Conservation | Creative Kids |

# Unit 4-11

# Printable Pack

This unit includes printables at the end. To make life easier for you we also created digital printable packs for each unit. To retrieve your printable pack for Unit 4-11, please visit

www.layers-of-learning.com/digital-printable-packs/

Put the printable pack in your shopping cart and use this coupon code:

## 741UNIT4-11

Your printable pack will be free.

# Layers of Learning Introduction

This is part of a series of units in the Layers of Learning homeschool curriculum, including the subjects of history, geography, science, and the arts. Children from 1st through 12th can participate in the same curriculum at the same time - family school style.

The units are intended to be used in order as the basis of a complete curriculum (once you add in a systematic math, reading, and writing program). You begin with Year 1 Unit 1 no matter what ages your children are. Spend about 2 weeks on each unit. You pick and choose the activities within the unit that appeal to you and read the books from the book list that are available to you or find others on the same topic from your library. We highly recommend that you use the timeline in every history section as the backbone. Then flesh out your learning with reading and activities that highlight the topics you think are the most important.

Alternatively, you can use the units as activity ideas to supplement another curriculum in any order you wish. You can still use them with all ages of children at the same time.

When you've finished with Year One, move on to Year Two, Year Three, and Year Four. Then begin again with Year One and work your way through the years again. Now your children will be older, reading more involved books, and writing more in depth. When you have completed the sequence for the second time, you start again on it for the third and final time. If your student began with Layers of Learning in 1st grade and stayed with it all the way through she would go through the four year rotation three times, firmly cementing the information in her mind in ever increasing depth. At each level you should expect increasing amounts of outside reading and writing. High schoolers in particular should be reading extensively, and if possible, participating in discussion groups.

These icons will guide you in spotting activities and books that are appropriate for the age of child you are working with. But if you think an activity is too juvenile or too difficult for your kids, adjust accordingly. The icons are not there as rules, just guides.

☺ 1st-4th
☻ 5th-8th
☻ 9th-12th

Within each unit we share:

EXPLORATIONS, activities relating to the topic;
EXPERIMENTS, usually associated with science topics;
EXPEDITIONS, field trips;
EXPLANATIONS, teacher helps or educational philosophies.

In the sidebars we also include Additional Layers, Famous Folks, Fabulous Facts, On the Web, and other extra related topics that can take you off on tangents, exploring the world and your interests with a bit more freedom. The curriculum will always be there to pull you back on track when you're ready.

www.layers-of-learning.com

# UNIT ELEVEN

## WORLD WAR II - SYMBOLS & LANDMARKS - AIR & WATER - WAR ART

*The true sign of intelligence is not knowledge, but imagination.*
-Albert Einstein

## LIBRARY LIST

**HISTORY**

Search for: World War II, Winston Churchill, Adolf Hitler, Joseph Stalin, Franklin Delano Roosevelt, Holocaust, Miracle at Dunkirk, Battle of Britain, Vimey Ridge, Bataan, Douglas MacArthur

☺ The Little Ships: The Heroic Rescue at Dunkirk by Louise Borden.

☺ The Greatest Skating Race by Louise Borden.

☺ Forging Freedom by Hudson Talbott. True story of real heroism.

☺ The Unbreakable Code by Sara Hunter.

☺ Baseball Saved Us by Ken Mochizuki. True story of a Japanese internment camp.

☺ ☻ Snow Treasure by Marie McSwiggen. True story of heroic Norwegian children.

☺ ☻ When Hitler Stole Pink Rabbit by Judith Kerr.

☺ ☻ Number the Stars by Lois Lowry. Fictional account of real events.

☻ World War II by Tim McGowan. Brief overview of the European front.

☻ World War II: An Interactive History Adventure by Elizabeth Raum.

☻ We Were Heroes by Walter Dean Meyers. A fictional "journal" from a soldier.

☺ The Battle of the Bulge by Bill Cain. Graphic history; look for others in the series.

☺ Rosie the Riveter by Penny Colman.

☻ Lost Childhood: My Life In A Japanese Internment Camp by Annelex Hofstra Layson. True story. Some parts are disturbing, pre-read and discuss with your child.

☻ Hidden on the Mountain by Karen Ruelle and Deborah Desaix. A gem.

☻ Going Solo by Roald Dahl. His real life adventures as a WWII pilot.

☺ ☻ The Endless Steppe by Esther Hautzig. Based on the author's own experience of being arrested and shipped from Poland to Siberia by the Russians during WWII.

☺ ☻ Diary of A Young Girl by Anne Frank. Classic, a must-read.

☺ ☻ World War II by Simon Adams. From DK.

☺ ☻ The Good Fight: How World War II Was Won by Stephen E. Ambrose.

☺ ☻ Surviving Hitler by Andrea Warren. True story of a concentration camp.

☻ On Hitler's Mountain: Overcoming the Legacy of a Nazi Childhood by Irmgard Hunt.

☻ The Hiding Place by Corrie Ten Boom. Excellent, but has some disturbing parts.

☻ Night by Elie Wiesel. Also disturbing. Compare to *The Hiding Place*.

☻ World War II: The Rest of The Story and How It Affects You Today by Richard J. Maybury.

☺ A Short History of World War II by James L. Stokesbury. Readable WWII from causes to aftermath in one volume. Objective tone.

| | |
|---|---|
| **GEOGRAPHY** | Search for: United States symbols, White House, Statue of Liberty, Washington Monument, Lincoln Memorial, American flag, specific names of landmarks that interest you<br><br>☺ ☻ ☻ How To Draw Cartoon Symbols of the United States of America by Curt Visca.<br><br>☺ Oh, Say Can You See?: America's Symbols, Landmarks, and Important Words by Sheila Keenan.<br><br>☺ The Pledge of Allegiance by Scholastic.<br><br>☺ F is for Flag by Wendy Cheyette Lewison.  Look for others by this author.<br><br>☺ The Bald Eagle by Lloyd G. Douglas.  Easy reader.  Look for others in this series.<br><br>☺ The Great Seal of the United States by Norman Pearl.<br><br>☺ Our Flag by Carl Memling.  A Little Golden Book.<br><br>☺ ☻ The Story of the Statue of Liberty by Betsy and Guilio Maestro.<br><br>☺ ☻ Money, Money, Money: The Meaning of the Art and Symbols on United States Currency by Nancy Winslow Parker.<br><br>☺ ☻ Celebrate America: Guide to America's Sights and Symbols by Norman Pearl and Mary Firestone.<br><br>☺ ☻ Red, White, Blue, and Uncle Who? by Theresa Bateman.  All the major symbols.<br><br>☻ ☻ Why the Turkey Didn't Fly: The Surprising Stories Behind the Eagle, the Flag, Uncle Sam, and Other Images of America by Paul Aron.<br><br>☻ The Statue of Liberty: A Transatlantic Story by Edward Berenson.<br><br>☻ To The Flag by Richard J. Ellis.  Tells of the history and controversy surrounding the Pledge of Allegiance.<br><br>☻ The United States Capitol: Its Architecture and Decoration by Henry Hope Reed.<br><br>☻ We The People: The Story of the United States Capitol by Lonnelle Aikman. |
| **SCIENCE** | Search for: chemistry of air, chemistry of water, atmosphere, oceans (steer clear of environmentalist books and focus on books that teach composition and chemistry for this unit)<br><br>☻ Atmosphere: Sea of Air by Roy A. Gallant.<br><br>☺ ☻ Water Science Fair Projects by Madeline P. Goodstein.<br><br>☺ ☻ How Did We Find Out About the Atmosphere? by Isaac Asimov.<br><br>☺ ☻ Oceans and Atmosphere by Globe Pearson.<br><br>☻ The Alchemy of Air by Thomas Hager.  The story of how nitrogen was grabbed from the air and turned into food to feed the world by the crackpot scientist who was also a Jewish eugenicist for Hitler during WWII.  Crazy stuff, fascinating read. |
| **THE ARTS** | Search for: Wartime art, Dada, war artists, war photographers<br><br>☺ ☻ ☻ Draw 50 Airplanes, Aircraft, and Spacecraft by Lee J. Ames.  Has war aircraft.<br><br>☺ ☻ ☻ The Art of War by Sean Stewart Price.  Teaches history with art.<br><br>☺ ☻ ☻ World War II Posters: 24 Cards from Dover.  Art postcards.<br><br>☻ Civil War Witness: Matthew Brady's Photos Reveal the Horrors of War by Don Nardo and Bob Zeller.<br><br>☻ Leaving China: An Artist Paints His World War II Childhood by James McMullan. |

# HISTORY: WORLD WAR II

World War II began with the reparations after World War I. The Germans had been given harsh treatment. They were so totally demoralized and poverty stricken that when a young idealist came along who could promise a renewed hope and strength and an appropriately vague brighter future, they embraced him without ever understanding what he was really saying.

Meanwhile, World War I with its modern machines, modern guns, modern gas, and modern bombs had been a truly horrific experience for Europe. In response, many people, including the leaders of nations, embraced pacifism as a policy and urged appeasement toward belligerent parties. They were totally unprepared morally or physically for an aggressor like Adolf Hitler, who they were unwittingly encouraging.

At the start of World War II Adolf Hitler aimed his rather weak forces at France in the west and at Poland in the east. Both were overrun within weeks while putting up only a paltry defense. The concentration camps were already set up, and Hitler began shipping Polish, Dutch, Austrian, Danish, and French Jews and other undesirables to death camps.

*Hitler reviewing his troops in the spring of 1932.*

The British attempted to come to the aid of their allies, including little Belgium, but the British had failed to prepare too, Winston Churchill being almost the only voice of reason. The British and French troops became trapped on a little peninsula on the coast called Dunkirk. The entire resistance movement would fail if they perished. The British mobilized every boat they could find from navy destroyers to little fishing boats and rich men's yachts and succeeded in rescuing more than 335,000 men from the beaches over the course of nine days in order to prepare and fight another day.

For the next four years Britain, the United States, Russia, Australia, Canada and the freedom fighters of overrun European nations barely held on against the aggressors of Germany and Italy. Slowly the Allies built up their war machine, got organized, and began the push back, landing on the beaches of Normandy in June of 1944. By the spring of 1945 Allied troops were entering Germany, and the Americans were poised on the southern islands of Japan. In August of 1945 the atomic bombs had been dropped on Japan, ending the bloodiest war in history. Over 60 million soldiers and civilians all over the world died as a result of the war. About 4% of the population of the entire world at that time died from combat, bombing raids, disease, famine, ethnic cleansing, and other causes directly related to the war. Germany lost approximately 10% of her population.

### ☺ ☺ ☺ EXPLORATION: Timeline

There are printable timeline squares at the end of this unit. Place the timeline squares on a wall timeline or in a notebook timeline, discussing them as you go. This timeline is long and takes place in just a few years so you may want to create a "pop-out' timeline of World War II. The events in this timeline show how the Nazis gained power and then how the Allies fought back and regained lost territory.

### ☺ ☺ EXPLORATION: Miracle at Dunkirk

As the Germans relentlessly advanced across Belgium, the French and British hastily organized a resistance and sent troops in opposition. The Allied troops were hopelessly pinned down at Dunkirk after spectacularly losing the battle. Bombed night and day from the Luftwaffe flying overhead and fending off constant attacks from the land, the entire British and French resistance was about to die before it had even begun.

On the 26th of May, 1940 King George VI called for a week of prayer, and Winston Churchill began to mobilize a rescue operation, code-named Operation Dynamo.

With a force of only 40,000 French soldiers, General Molinié held back seven German divisions for four days at the city of Lille as other British and French troops held the line around the beaches so the British troops could organize their escape. On the first day, only about 7,000 men were loaded onto boats. But by the ninth

**Memorization Station**

The main Axis powers were Germany, Japan, and Italy. The Allies included Great Britain, the U.S., China, France, Australia, the Soviet Union, Canada, and many other countries.

**Additional Layer**

Japan invaded China in 1937. They killed over 100,000 people, mostly unarmed civilians, in Nanking alone. This event became known as the "Rape of Nanking." By 1938, the Japanese controlled most of the populated areas of China. But a resistance movement was underway, led by a young military officer called Mao Zedong. The war would continue until 1945 when the Americans bombed and subdued Japan.

**Additional Layer**

By 1935, German Jews were already being severely persecuted. The jobs they could hold were restricted. It was illegal to marry outside their race. Their children could not attend school. They had to live in Ghetto neighborhoods specifically set aside for them. And they all wore a yellow star.

## Fabulous Fact

Japan was threatening the entire Pacific, including Australia, which had sent most of its troops and equipment to Europe for the fight against Germany. Australia was almost completely dependent on the U.S. for protection.

*Australian troops in England in 1940.*

## Additional Layer

The Spanish Civil War was fought between the socialists and the fascists in Spain from 1936 to 1939.

The Fascists allied with Germany and Italy and practiced unrestricted warfare against civilians. The fascists won, installing Francisco Franco as dictator where he stayed until his death in 1975.

After his death the monarchy and a republican form of government were restored.

Read more about the Spanish Civil War.

day more than 335,000 men had been rescued off the beaches and from the harbor. Many of the men waded out into shoulder deep water, waiting for hours for their turn to board a boat.

933 boats of every possible description had been assembled voluntarily by the British people. Many of the little boats were used as ferries to take the men out to the larger transport ships. Merchant ships, fishing ships, lifeboats, flat bottomed Dutch coasters, pleasure craft, and government vessels all assisted at their peril. Meanwhile the Germans bombed from the skies and from shore, the seas were patrolled by German destroyers, and mines were set to interfere with British ships. Over 200 of the Allied craft were sunk during the operation.

Besides the troops fighting on the land and the ships fighting from the water, the British sent their Royal Air Force pilots to cover the retreating troops and counter the Luftwaffe. 177 RAF planes went down during the operation over Dunkirk, but the RAF destroyed 262 German planes over the nine days.

Two French divisions remained behind to cover the retreat. They held out just long enough and then were destroyed, the survivors surrendering on June 3, 1940 and remaining prisoners of war to the end.

The day after the operation, Churchill gave a speech calling the evacuation effort a "miracle." The British press spun the horrific defeat into a victory for the British people and emphasized how strong and resilient the British could be if they worked together as a nation, civilian and military. Dunkirk boosted the British morale and prepared them for the next trial, the Battle of Britain.

At the end of this unit you will find a printable game board "WWII: Miracle At Dunkirk" and printable troop cards. Print the troop cards on card stock and cut apart. Print the game board. Color the water blue, Allied areas red, and German areas green. You can give each child his or her own game board or play as a group, taking turns rolling. Place the cards near Dunkirk in the Allied control area. The object of the game is to get as many of your troops off of the beach as you can before the Germans kill them all. You will roll two or more dice. For each die that is even, move a troop card to the water and then to the safety of England. Each card must move twice, by rolling even numbers each time, before it will be safe. For every die that is odd, remove one of your cards from play; those soldiers have been killed. As you roll the dice, each die counts individually as an even or an odd.

## ☺ ☺ ☺ EXPLORATION: Battle of Britain

After the Germans overran the Netherlands, Belgium, and France, the only opponent left in the west was Britain. In the east Russia was feebly resisting, and everywhere else was Nazi occupied. The Germans began an air war, bombing Britain.

Britain churned out 300 new planes every week and sent up barely trained, new pilots who might last one or, if they were lucky, two or three flights before going down. The attacks started in July of 1940. By October it was clear the British could not be subdued and would never surrender. The Battle of Britain was won. The Germans would never invade, though they would bomb England throughout the war.

Winston Churchill summed up the importance of the battle and the sacrifice of the young men who went knowingly to their deaths to protect their homeland and families: "Never in the field of human conflict was so much owed by so many to so few." Listen to Churchill's whole speech: http://youtu.be/-57Q_hSAUeU

Print model airplanes of WWII and this battle here: http://layers-of-learning.com/world-war-ii-printable-planes-battle-britain/. Learn more about the planes and the pilots.

### On the Web
The BBC has an interactive WWII site for kids. http://www.bbc.co.uk/schools/primaryhistory/world_war2/

### Additional Layer

The Reichstag Building was the seat of government in Germany for several hundred years. It burned in 1933, giving Hitler an excuse to institute emergency powers and take over the government.

*The Reichstag government building in Berlin.*

Other governments during WWII would use the same excuse, an emergency, to take illegal actions.

The Americans, for example, illegally detained Japanese and German Americans and placed them in internment camps for the duration of the war.

Think about the purpose of law. When, if ever, should the law be suspended?

## On The Web

Paper soldiers, tanks, air-planes and ships to print and play: www.junior-general.org/index.php/figure/figureList/ww2

And here's a paper tank to print and put together:

http://papertoys.com/tank.htm

### Fabulous Fact

The German air force was called the Luftwaffe (Luft-wof-uh). Though illegal according to the Versailles Treaty, the Luftwaffe was formed in Germany in 1935 and, by the start of the war, they were the best equipped and trained air force in the world, having gained experience during the Spanish Civil War.

### On the Web

Watch this WWII quick synopsis from John Green.

http://youtu.be/Q78COTwT7nE

Mr. Green gives some ideas about why he thinks the war happened. Talk it over.

### ☺ ☺ ☺ EXPLORATION: Pearl Harbor Lei

Early in the morning of December 7, 1941, Japanese fighter planes flew over the island of Oahu, bombing and strafing military targets. First, they went for the airfields at Hickam, Wheeler, Bellows, and Ford Island where the planes were conveniently and neatly lined up out in the open to prevent sabotage. The plan was to disable and destroy any hope of air resistance to the attack. Then the Japanese bombers went for the naval docking in Pearl Harbor itself. There was almost no resistance from the totally surprised Americans. 353 Japanese fighters and bombers destroyed eighteen ships, including five battle ships, 188 planes with another 159 damaged, and killed 2,402 soldiers, wounding another 1,282.

At the time of the attack, the United States and Japan were actively in the midst of peace talks, and Japan failed to declare war or cease the talks beforehand. This led the U.S. president, Franklin D. Roosevelt, to say December 7, 1941 is "a date which will live in infamy." The United States formally declared war on Japan on December 8, thirty three minutes after President Roosevelt gave his "Infamy" speech. Germany and Italy then declared war on the United States and the U.S. reciprocated, joining the war in Europe and the Pacific at the same time.

Watch this short clip of the attack and the speech by Roosevelt: http://youtu.be/3VqQAf74fsE

Then make a remembrance lei using the printable at the end of this unit. Print the lei flowers onto heavy paper, color them, and cut them out. Use a needle to string them together alternating with pieces of cut straws.

### ☺ ☺ ☺ EXPLORATION: Bataan Collage

The Philippines, under protection of the United States, was attacked the same day as Pearl Harbor. Like Pearl Harbor, the first targets were the airfields. The air forces were rendered useless and without air support. With the Navy decimated at Pearl Harbor, the islands were wide open to a ground invasion. On December 22, 1941, the main ground assault began. The U.S. and Filipino troops started a fighting retreat toward the Bataan Peninsula, which they planned to hold until the U.S. could organize a relief effort. They hoped to hold out for six months. But soon it became apparent that the U.S. would not be able to fight their way there for perhaps two years or more.

The capital city of Manila fell on December 24 and, except for Bataan, the Japanese controlled the islands. The Americans and Filipinos held out on Bataan under constant fire. Short of food and supplies, exhausted and emaciated, they finally negotiated a surrender on April 9, 1942.

What happened next is the real story. 60,000 Filipino and 15,000 American soldiers were taken prisoner and force marched 80 miles to a prison camp in the interior of the island. On the way they were given little to no food and only dirty water to drink. The Japanese soldiers beat, taunted, bayoneted, beheaded, and shot their captives at will and often with no provocation. The Japanese believed that any who surrendered had lost all honor and were thus to be treated shamefully. In all, at least 3,000, and perhaps as many as 10,000, men were killed while on the march. Once the prison camp was reached, the brutality continued as soldiers died of hunger, disease, and abuse.

Make a collage page for your notebook. Search for images of WWII soldiers; you can focus on the soldiers of Bataan, the Pacific Theater, or any WWII photos. You may want to include a black and white image of the POW/MIA flag. Print out some of your favorites and cover a piece of card stock, leaving no white space.

## Famous Folks

The success of British air defense can be put down to one man, Hugh Dowding, who was probably the only person in the world who believed bombers could be defended against and therefore set out to do it. Learn more.

## On the Web

This excellent 40-minute documentary explains the Battle of Britain.

http://youtu.be/RAuT_-wC7nw

## Library List

These are all good (and clean) World War II movies for the family.

Miracle of the White Stallions (1963)

The Sound of Music (1965)

Battle of the Bulge (1965)

Sands of Iwo Jima (1949)

The Longest Day (1962)

Sink the Bismark (1960)

Midway (1976)

Operation Pacific (1951)

Flying Tigers (1942)

The Great Escape (1963)

Millions Like Us (1943)

Casablanca (1942)

Battle of Britain (1969)

The Dirty Dozen (1967)

## Fabulous Fact

LEAVE THIS TO US SONNY — **YOU** OUGHT TO BE OUT OF LONDON

MINISTRY OF HEALTH EVACUATION SCHEME

Operation Pied Piper was the removal of children from London and other large towns to the countryside to protect them from the bombing raids. It began during the Battle of Britain.

## Additional Layer

Japanese Americans and Canadians were forcibly moved to camps, complete with barbed wire and armed guard towers during the war.

These people were citizens, but were treated as criminals. Read Executive Order 9066 for yourself: http://www.ourdocuments.gov/doc.php?flash=true&doc=74

## ☺ ☻ EXPLORATION: The Home Front

This war didn't just involve the soldiers who marched off to the front. It was total war and required the efforts and sacrifices of whole nations. Moms went to work in the factories to build airplanes, bombs, guns, jeeps, tanks and military supplies of every kind. The women also worked in the fields, planting and harvesting crops, milking the cows, and running the shops of every town while most of the men were away.

At the end of this unit you'll find a printable "We Can Do It" Rosie the Riveter coloring sheet to add to your notebook.

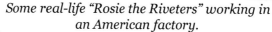

*Some real-life "Rosie the Riveters" working in an American factory.*

## ☺ ☻ EXPLORATION: Rationing

Many items were rationed as the war effort took off. Every family received a book of stamps or tickets, and they took their tickets to the store and were allowed to buy only as much as they had tickets for. Rationed items included gasoline, nylons, sugar, meat, silk, shoes, tires, eggs, and many other items.

Read more about rationing here: www.ameshistory.org/content/world-war-ii-rationing-us-homefront

Print out the ration book and stamps from the end of this unit. Fold and glue the ration book cover, and glue it onto a notebook page. Then insert your coupons. Go "shopping" in your kitchen for the ingredients you'll need. But remember, your rations have to last all week.

Lord Woolton's Pie

- In season vegetables like carrots, turnips, cauliflower, beans, potatoes, and onions
- Potatoes for mashing
- 2 Tbsp. flour
- 1 Tbsp. butter
- 1 ½ cups milk
- cheddar, grated
- sage or thyme for sauce
- salt
- pepper

1. Peel the potatoes; save the peelings for roasting in the oven later with salt and herbs. Nothing was wasted during the war.
2. Cut up and cook the potatoes in boiling water until soft and ready to mash.
3. Mash the potatoes with ½ cup milk and some salt (no butter, it was rationed and the little bit you have will go into your sauce).
4. Prepare, dice, and cook the in season vegetables in salted water until tender.
5. Drain the water off the veggies and place into a pie dish.
6. Mix the butter and flour in a saucepan, then add 1 cup milk slowly while stirring over medium heat. Add in pepper, herbs, and salt to taste. Stir until thickened and bubbly.
7. Pour sauce over vegetables.
8. Place the mashed potatoes into a baggie with a small hole cut in the corner and pipe on top of the veggies and sauce.
9. Sprinkle grated cheese over the top.
10. Bake at 350° F for 20 minutes, or until the cheese is melted and browned.

This dish was created by the Savoy Hotel, London during the war, touted by the War Ministry as a healthy ration-friendly dish, and named after Britain's Minister of Food.

### ☺ ☺ EXPLORATION: D-Day
On June 6, 1944, the Allied forces landed in France and began to push back against the German onslaught. D-day began just after midnight with an airborne landing of 24,000 British, Canadian, and American paratroopers. At 6:30 in the morning, 160,000 soldiers made an amphibious landing with the aid of 195,700 naval personnel in over 5,000 ships. It was the most enormous undertaking of its kind ever and a complete surprise to the Germans.

But it was far from easy. The Germans had heavily entrenched defenses along every coast, including at Normandy. And though there were pre-assault bombing runs designed to clear some of the German defenses and guns, many of these went wrong. At the Omaha Beach landing site, the bombers had dropped their ordinance too far inland, leaving the coastal defenses intact. Some of the boats swamped or leaked. Some of the boats couldn't get close enough to shore. The men were under heavy fire, fighting to clear the beaches of mines and obstacles so further troops could be landed. Omaha was defended by the elite 352nd German Infantry division, trained and placed there by Rommel himself who suspected an Allied landing was imminent. Rommel ordered the troops to defend Omaha Beach with buried stakes, mines, fenc-

## Famous Folks
General Douglas MacArthur was the commander of the United States forces in the Philippines.

He oversaw the Battle of Bataan and was unwillingly evacuated from the Philippines in March. After reaching Australia he gave a statement to the press directed toward the Philippine people, who he had served and loved, promising them, "I shall return." He did. Two years later he drove the Japanese from the island. He is a national hero in the Philippines.

## Writer's Workshop
Choose one of these topics and make a poster board presentation:

Tuskegee Airmen, Higgins Boat, War Time Espionage, The GI Bill, Navajo Code Talkers, Women's Army Corps, the 1936 Olympic Games, or the Manhattan Project.

Present it to a group.

## Fabulous Fact

Most of America's rubber came from Dutch plantations in the East Indies. They were seized by Japan immediately following the attack on Pearl Harbor. Rubber was in short supply and desperately needed for military vehicles. Many people rode bicycles with no tires until the war was over.

*This is a Malaysian rubber plantation burning as the British retreat to Singapore.*

## Additional Layer

Try this WWII cake:

1 ¾  cup flour
1 ½ cup sugar
1 tsp. baking soda
3 Tbsp. baking cocoa
½ tsp. salt
1 tsp. vanilla
1 ½ cup water
½ cup oil

Mix right in your greased baking pan. Bake at 375°F for 30 minutes. Top with powdered sugar.

es, wire, and something nicknamed "Rommel's asparagus" by his troops. They were tall wooden posts with artillery shells balanced on top which would explode if hit, preventing gliders from strategically crashing.

Eventually a few isolated pockets of men, working in small independent groups, secured a few paths and defensive positions from which the troops could branch out and secure more land. The Allies had a foothold. At least 12,000 Allied troops died or were wounded during the D-Day landings.

At the end of this unit you will find a Soldier's Medals Printable. These are actual medals given to Allied soldiers during WWII. Learn a little about each medal. Print them, cut them out, and award them to your kids during this unit for things like "heroically removing the trash," "Bravery in the face of a dirty bathroom," or "services to the family." You can then paste your medals to your soldier's uniform printable (also at the end of this unit) and put it in your notebook.

## ☺ ☺ ☻ EXPLORATION: Battle of the Bulge

Firmly entrenched in France, the Allies had the Germans on the run. This made them dangerously overconfident, stretched thin, and under supplied by lines that couldn't keep up. The Germans, in a last ditch attempt to save the situation, had planned a final big push and covertly moved their tanks into the forest of the Ardennes. But the Allies thought the Germans were preparing defensive operations only, and those far from the quiet Ardennes Forest. Only U.S. Colonel Oscar Koch, an intelligence officer, predicted the Germans were planning a major offensive in the forest. No one believed he was right, but General Patton did create a contingency plan in case Koch's prediction came true.

A week before the battle started, a small contingent of English speaking Germans, wearing U.S. military uniforms, infiltrated enemy lines and changed signposts, seized bridges across the Meuse, and generally created as much confusion as possible. Their ultimate plan was to try and assassinate General Eisenhower, but they were caught before they achieved that objective.

The full attack started at 5:30 A.M. on December 16. The Germans began with an artillery barrage along an 80 mile front. Then the Germans charged forward, rapidly taking villages, bridges, and crossroads in their push west. Their forward movement made an inward bulge in the Allied lines. That is where the name for the battle, coined by the press, came from.

The Allies were pushing back by the 26th of December. Bastogne was relieved, and the Germans were losing tanks and men to Allied bullets, hunger, exhaustion, and fuel and ammunition shortages. On January 1, the Germans launched one last air assault, throwing everything they had at Allied air fields. The Luftwaffe losses in this attack left them weak for the rest of the war while the Allied air forces were constantly resupplied with fuel, planes, and pilots. The Germans were finished off due to supply problems more than any other single factor.

### Additional Layer

Grow a victory garden like kids and moms during World War II. You might also practice reusing and recycling everything for a week or two while you do this unit. What if you couldn't go to the store to get new socks, plastic bags, or tires for your bike? What if your dad's life depended on getting enough aluminum to build planes or lead to make bullets?

### On the Web

President Roosevelt began giving periodic "Fireside Chats" during the Great Depression. The radio addresses continued throughout the war. millercenter.org/the-presidency/presidential-speeches/february-23-1942-fireside-chat-20-progress-war

### Famous Folks

The American General Dwight D. Eisenhower was the Supreme Allied Commander during the war. Later his popularity would win him the White House.

The battle was over on January 25th, 1945. The Germans were retreating, making their way back home as well as they could. They had abandoned most of their equipment and guns. Casualties included 84,834 Germans, 89,500 Americans with 19,000 killed, 1,408 British with 200 killed, and 3,000 civilians killed.

Color a map of the European conflict from the end of this unit. Color the map to show the greatest extent of German-controlled territory, the Allies, and the neutral states. Also shown on the

## Additional Layer

The invasion at Normandy was a surprise, mostly because the Germans were fooled by several ruses, including Operation Bodyguard. The Germans were misled into thinking the invasion would happen at a different time and place. Throughout the war, the Allies were the masters of intelligence, with operatives continually sending good information from behind German lines. Meanwhile, many German operatives who were sent to Britain turned traitor and became double agents.

## Famous Folks

Erwin Rommel was the commander of the German armored units. His brilliant leadership was instrumental to German success through the war.

## On the Web

Listen to "Songs That Got Us Through WWII" play list on YouTube. Look up songs from around the world.

map are the Nazi Death Camps; color these. Besides the death camps there were hundreds of concentration camps everywhere from Norway to Southern France and from Greece to the Ukraine, besides those in Germany itself; these are not shown on the map. The battles shown on the map are all Allied victories, and most happened in the second half of the war after the Germans had overreached and failed to secure sources of oil and supplies. Use the map to aid in coloring.

## ☺ ☺ ☺ EXPLORATION: Okinawa and Iwo Jima

On the same day the Japanese attacked Pearl Harbor, they attacked the Philippines, Indonesia, and dozens of other Pacific Islands. The occupations were a total surprise to the western powers who ruled most of Asia at that time. The Dutch, the English, the French, the Americans, the Portuguese, and others were completely overrun and most stayed occupied until the Japanese surrender in 1945.

The U.S. mobilized their Navy and Marines rapidly and began the push back. Midway Island was taken in June of 1942, six months after the war began. The U.S. strategy after that was to "island hop," retaking islands one at a time, moving ever closer to the Japanese main islands, which would be taken last of all.

In February of 1945, the Marines took the heavily defended island of Iwo Jima, the first of the Japanese home islands to be taken, after more than a month of heavy fighting. The American losses were horrific, nearly a third of the 70,000 men were killed or wounded. The Japanese losses were even more horrifying and gave the Americans a taste of what they could expect from here on out in the war. The Japanese soldiers did not surrender. They kept fighting to the death even after being mortally wounded. Of the 22,060 Japanese soldiers on the island only 216 were taken prisoner, those being unconscious or otherwise incapacitated, while the rest were killed to a man.

Okinawa was the same story, except Okinawa was not a barren island used only for military operations as Iwo Jima was. Okinawa was home to several hundred thousand Japanese civilians who had all been told by their government to resist to the death and to commit suicide rather than surrender. The fighting lasted for 82 days and claimed the lives of over 100,000 Japanese soldiers and perhaps as many as 150,000 civilians, most of whom committed suicide. American casualties, killed and wounded, added up to 65,000. Americans were forced to make war on old men, women, and even children armed with nothing more than shovels, sticks, and their bare hands.

Color a map of the Pacific Theater. Show Japanese territory and battle victories in red. Show Allied territories and American victories in blue.

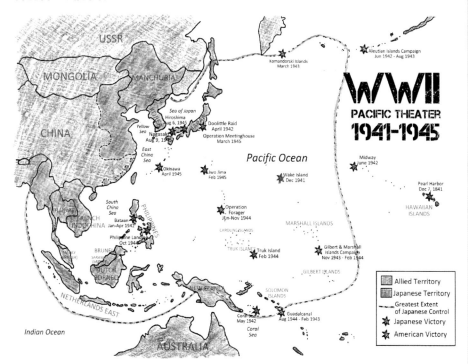

☺ ☺ ☻ **EXPLORATION: Holocaust**

About 12 million people were killed in work camps and concentration camps or just lined up and shot in front of their homes by the Nazis during and just before the war. About half of them were Jews. The others were cripples, gypsies, resistance fighters, homosexuals, or anyone who spoke out or was accused of speaking out against the Nazis.

Hitler's determined extermination of the Jewish race is called the Holocaust. Read more about the Holocaust. In remembrance of those who died or suffered at the hands of the Nazis, draw a six pointed star on a sheet of paper. Color it yellow like the stars the Jews were forced to wear to single them out. Color the outline of the star in black and draw on barbs, like the wire that imprisoned the Jews. Finally, choose a quote from Elie Weisel, a Holocaust survivor and writer, to copy onto your paper.

☺ ☻ **EXPLORATION: Counting the Cost**

Research information on how many people died during WWII. Find out how many died in concentration camps and as prisoners of war. Discuss the consequences of a German victory. What would have happened to Europe and to the rest of the world? Discuss whether fighting back was worth the lives lost.

**Additional Layer**

On the second day of battle, 150 lightly armed American soldiers surrendered. They were brought to a crossroads near Malmedy and placed under guard. Some SS troops arrived and opened fire on the prisoners, massacring 84 of them. Some escaped and took the tale back to the American lines where outrage ensued.

After the massacre at Malmedy, American unit commanders told their troops to "take no prisoners." In at least one incident, at Chenogne, Belgium, German soldiers were executed by their American captors.

**Additional Layer**

The Japanese surrendered when the U.S. dropped two atomic bombs. "Little Boy" was dropped on Hiroshima and 3 days later "Fat Man" was dropped on Nagasaki. The effects were devastating and long-lasting. Learn more about these sad events.

# GEOGRAPHY: SYMBOLS & LANDMARKS

America has some important symbols that create a national identity and help the people to feel pride in the things that are great about the country. These symbols include things like the flag and the bald eagle, and also places like Thomas Jefferson's home, the Washington Monument, and the Statue of Liberty.

One of the unique aspects of American symbols is that we usually think of them as representing the people and the ideals of America rather than representing the government itself. For example, the Statue of Liberty does not represent the government. It represents the concept that America is a refuge of liberty and a light for an oppressed world.

### ☻ ☻ ☻ EXPLORATION: The Flag

A flag is a symbol of a country and often also a symbol of what that country stands for. America's flag has thirteen red and white stripes, representing the original 13 colonies, and a field of blue with fifty white stars, one for each state. But that's not what the flag stands for. When people see the American flag they think about freedom, hope, opportunity, love, human dignity, justice, equality, and righteous government.

Because the flag stands for such important, honorable, and sacred things, people ought to always treat the flag with respect. Here are some rules abut the flag that everyone should know:

1. A flag should not be allowed to touch the ground, be crumpled on a shelf or stuffed in a box, be torn, be dirty, or be treated in any other disrespectful manner.
2. When a flag is displayed outside, it should be taken down at night or a spotlight should be shone on it.
3. The American flag is always flown higher and to the right of the

flags of other countries or state flags when on U.S. soil.

4. The flag is displayed with the stars on the hoist side (the left side). A flag flown upside down is a symbol of distress.

5. During a flag ceremony, always stand and place your hand on your heart (or salute if you are in uniform) as the flag is carried to the front and posted or hoisted on a pole. Not everyone knows these rules so you may be one of the few standing at first. Be a good example.

6. When a flag gets old and worn out, dispose of it in a formal retiring ceremony. This is usually done by burning the flag. First it is folded in a triangle then completely burned while the audience stands at attention with their hands over their hearts. Then the ashes are completely buried.

Learn to hold a flag ceremony at your house and practice flag etiquette. Below we explain one simple ceremony you can do with your kids.

First you'll need a flag and a place to post it or hoist it. Then choose someone to be the leader and someone to carry the colors (the flag). You can also have additional people acting as the color guard and walking behind the person carrying the flag.

The leader stands at the front and says:

1. Will the audience please rise?
2. Color Guard, advance and post the colors.* (The color guard comes forward and posts the colors in your flag stand. If you are using more than the American flag, the American flag is always placed first and other flags afterward. As the flag is brought forward and posted, the audience should salute the flag by putting their right hands over their hearts. The color guard should join the salute as soon as they have posted the colors. Continue saluting until the audience is seated.)
3. *O flag of our Union,*
   *To you we'll be true,*
   *To your red and white stripes,*
   *And your stars on the blue;*
   *The emblem of freedom,*
   *The symbol of right,*
   *We children salute you,*
   *O flag fair and bright!* **
4. Thank you. The audience may now be seated. Color guard dismissed.

*If you're raising the flag up a pole, say "hoist the colors."

**This is a poem that school children memorized and recited a

## Expedition

The Vietnam Veteran's Memorial is located at the National Mall.

War memorials are a way of remembering those who have sacrificed for the rest of us. They are very important to a nation's identity. Do you have a war memorial in your town? Go visit it.

## Fabulous Fact

Washington D.C. is the home of the Supreme Court Building.

The building is neoclassical, designed as a "temple of justice" in the 1930s. It represents the law and its preeminence in the United States.

century ago in American classrooms. You can substitute another poem or patriotic quote or thought. Here are some: http://www.usflag.org/poetry.html. Alternatively, you can have everyone recite the Pledge of Allegiance together or sing a patriotic song as a group.

## ☺ EXPLORATION: The National Mall

The National Mall and the streets surrounding it contain many buildings and memorials of significance in American history.

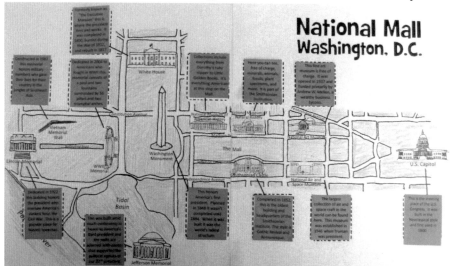

At the end of this unit you will find National Mall Cards and a two page map of the National Mall. Print the map, trim off the white space on the edge of one map so the two halves can be glued together and matched up. Then cut out the cards, read them, and glue them to the map in the spaces next to the memorial or building they describe. You should be able to tell from the descriptions where they belong, but if you're not sure, look it up. We printed our cards onto blue colored paper for visual interest. Then color the map. You can also look up photos and more information about the sites as you put them on your map.

## ☺ ☺ EXPLORATION: The Washington Monument

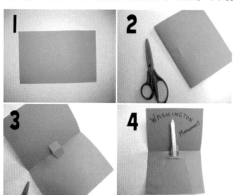

Make a pop-up monument card to open.

Start with a half sheet of paper. Fold it in half. Make two short cuts, about a half inch apart and centered, on the folded side of the paper. The notch you cut out becomes the place where you will mount your monument. Fold the notch back on itself. Draw the Washington Monument on paper, and cut it out. Mount it on the notch and add other background elements, gluing them to the original card surface.

While the kids work, tell them about the history of the monument and what it stands for.

### ☺ ☺ ☻ EXPLORATION: Arlington

Arlington National Cemetery is a military cemetery. It is located directly across the Potomac River from the Lincoln Memorial on the Robert E. Lee Estate, which was confiscated during the Civil War. Later, Lee's grandson, Custis Lee, sued the federal government for taking his land unconstitutionally. He won, was given back the land, and then sold it back to the government the following year.

To be buried at Arlington you have to have retired from the military, earned a high military honor, such as a purple heart or Medal of Honor, or been killed while on active duty. The requirements are more restrictive than at other military cemeteries because of the lack of burial space.

Besides the graves, there are also several memorials and tombs at Arlington, including the famous Tomb of the Unknown Soldier, a monument containing the bodies of unknown soldiers who could not be identified but who nevertheless deserve the highest honor. The tomb represents all those who were lost in battle, but never identified. The Tomb of the Unknown Soldier is guarded around the clock, 24-7, regardless of the weather, including during hurricanes, freezing temperatures and blistering heat, by the 3rd U.S. Infantry Regiment, called "The Old Guard."

Watch the Changing of the Guard here: http://youtu.be/L9rufM-BujMo

Make a model of Arlington Cemetery. Look up information on how the graves are laid out. Use a piece of cardboard, chipboard, or foam board as the base. Make rows of white grave stones from paper and write the names of some of the famous people buried there. Make a paper Tomb of the Unknown Soldier to add to your display.

### ☺ ☻ EXPLORATION: Statue of Liberty Costume

The Statue of Liberty is located on Liberty Island in New York Harbor. It was created by Frédéric Auguste Bartholdi and given to the United States of America as a gift from France in 1886. The statue has a broken chain at her feet, is holding a tablet of the

## Fabulous Fact

The first ever ticker tape parade was held in New York City at the opening of the Statue of Liberty. Long shredded paper, ticker tape, used to print off the running stock quotes in brokerage buildings, were thrown down from the upper stories of tall buildings onto the parade route. Ticker tape parades are reserved for important people who have done important things, sort of like the old Roman triumphal entries. If you get a ticker tape parade in your honor, you also get a plaque.

## On the Web

You can take a virtual tour of the Statue of Liberty and find out more about it here: http://www.nps.gov/stli/photosmultimedia/virtualtour.htm

## Fabulous Fact

The Jefferson Memorial celebrates Thomas Jefferson, one of the most prominent architects of freedom.

law, and is holding aloft a torch, all designed to show that liberty under the law is the ideal of both France and the United States.

Make a crown and torch to wear. Start with green construction paper. Color over it with a blue crayon to make the bluish-green color of the statue. Next cut two strips of the paper to make a headband. And from the rest, cut seven thin spikes. Tape the spikes to the headband.

To make the torch, cut three sheets of tissue paper into three 12" x 12" squares. Layer yellow, red, and orange. Grasp at the center of the papers and bunch them together. Stuff the bunched center down in a toilet paper tube, leaving the ends sticking out to make the flames.

## ☻ ☻ ☻ EXPLORATION: The Bald Eagle

The bald eagle was chosen by Congress as the national symbol in 1782 when the Great Seal was adopted. It represents freedom and strength.

Make a bald eagle pillowcase or t-shirt. Start with plain white fabric/pillowcase/t-shirt. Place a piece of cardboard under one layer of your fabric and smooth the fabric. Paint an eagle onto the fabric with fabric paints or draw with sharpie permanent markers. Young kids can use their handprints for the eagle's wings. The head can be shaped as a circle, the body as an oval. You can color the eagle in natural colors of brown and white or add in some red, white, and blue for patriotism.

☺ ☺ ☻ **EXPLORATION: Mt. Rushmore**

Mount Rushmore was sculpted between 1927 and 1941 by Gutson Borglum. It features the faces of four U.S. presidents - George Washington, Thomas Jefferson, Theodore Roosevelt, and Abraham Lincoln, carved in epic size onto the side of a granite cliff face.

Originally the plan had been to sculpt the faces of heroes of the west, like Lewis and Clark, Red Cloud, and Buffalo Bill, but the artist decided the sculpture ought to have more national appeal. It was carved to increase tourism to South Dakota. It worked. About 3 million people visit Mount Rushmore every year.

At the end of this unit you will find a printable Mount Rushmore, but without the faces drawn in. Have your kids decide who from American history they think deserves to be sculpted in gigantic proportions on the side of a mountain. Have them write a description of each person and why they chose those people to appear on the mountain side.

☺ ☺ ☻ **EXPLORATION: Liberty Bell**

The Liberty Bell is in Philadelphia near Independence Hall. It was commissioned for the Pennsylvania Colonial Hall, now Independence Hall, in 1752 and cast in London, England. It cracked

**Fabulous Fact**

Gateway Arch in St. Louis represents the westward migration of Americans during the 1800s and the city of St. Louis as the "Gateway to the West."

**Writer's Workshop**

Print out this coloring page with writing space (http://layers-of-learning.com/mount-rushmore-story-paper/) and have your kids write which president they think should be added to Mt. Rushmore and why.

**Additional Layer**

A private organization is carving a Crazy Horse Memorial not far from Mt. Rushmore. Learn more about the project.

*Photo by B24Canyns, CC by 4.0*

## Fabulous Fact

Independence Hall in Philadelphia was the location of the signing of the Declaration of Independence and later the drafting of the Constitution. It was built in 1753 to be the seat of government for the Pennsylvania colony. The Liberty Bell originally hung here.

## On the Web

Mt. Vernon was the home of George Washington, America's first and most important president.

You can take a virtual tour of the building here: http://www.mount-vernon.org/site/virtu-al-tour/

just after it reached Philadelphia the first time it was rung. It was recast twice in an attempt to repair it, but it cracked again in the early 1800s. An inscription on the bell reads "Proclaim LIBERTY throughout all the land unto all the inhabitants thereof. Leviticus 25: 10." The bell is a symbol of liberty, one of the cardinal virtues of the American form of government. Color the Liberty Bell printable from the end of this unit. Write the inscription on the bell.

## ☺ ☻ EXPLORATION: Great Seal of the United States

The United States has an official symbol which represents the government and is affixed to certain official papers like passports, military insignia, and official documents. This symbol is called the seal. There are two sides of the seal and therefore two designs. At the end of this unit you will find a coloring sheet of the Great Seal showing the designs from both sides and including fill in the blank questions about the seal. Use the information below to fill in the worksheet.

The eagle is clutching a sheaf of arrows in one talon and an olive branch in the other, symbolizing the desire of the government for peace, but the will and preparation for war, if necessary. The eagle's head is turned toward the olive branch, showing the preference for peace. There are thirteen arrows, thirteen olive leaves, and thirteen olives representing the thirteen original colonies. On a banner above the eagle are the Latin words E Pluribus Unum, which means, "Out of Many, One," meaning out of many separate states, one nation. Above the eagle is also a field of blue containing thirteen stars, again to represent the thirteen founding states. On the eagle's chest is a shield of thirteen red and white stripes which represent the separate thirteen states brought together and joined into one solid, unified whole. The red and white represent the congress and the blue above the stripes represents the president.

The reverse side of the seal shows a pyramid, representing

strength and duration, with an eye at the top of it. The pyramid has thirteen layers of stones representing the thirteen states. The eye represents the eye of Providence, or God, which is watching over the nation and in acknowledgment of the hand of God already seen in the formation of the nation by the founders. At the base of the pyramid are Roman numerals, 1776, the date of the Declaration of Independence. The words at the top say Annuit Cœptis, meaning "approves our undertakings," referring to God's approval. The words at the bottom say Novus ordo Seclorum, a phrase taken from Virgil, which means, "a new order of the ages."

☺ ☺ **EXPLORATION: Uncle Sam**

Uncle Sam is a character which represents the United States government. The story goes that during the War of 1812 boxes of meat sent to the troops were stamped with the initials "US." When the soldiers asked what it meant someone jokingly replied, "Uncle Sam." People started referring to the government as Uncle Sam. Cartoons of Uncle Sam were used as political statements in newspapers by the time of the Civil War. During World War I Uncle Sam was used by the government itself on recruitment posters.

Make an Uncle Sam treat bucket and fill it with patriotic yummies.

Start with a can, like from hot cocoa or coffee, or an ice cream bucket. If you have a metal can, make sure the metal edges inside the rim are not sharp. Paint the can all over in white as a base. It may take several coats; we recommend spray paint. Then give the kids acrylic paints and some images of Uncle Sam and let them

### Fabulous Fact

The Marine Corps War Memorial is located near Arlington Cemetery. It was crafted after a photo taken of marines raising the flag over Iwo Jima after they took the island during WWII.

### Fabulous Fact

Monticello was Thomas Jefferson's home. You can visit the house he designed himself.

### Additional Layer

For a patriotic treat to add to your Uncle Sam treat can, make your favorite sugar cookie recipe and divide it into thirds.

Add red food coloring to one third and blue food coloring to one third. Roll all three colors of dough into a thin rectangle and place them on top of one another. Roll up all three layers into a little log. Slice and bake.

# SCIENCE: AIR & WATER

## On the Web

Watch this old 1950's film about "The Properties of Air" before you start your experiments. https://www.youtube.com/watch?v=GyYUf1Zh1ZA

Have your kids take notes on the video. From the notes they can write 3-4 questions each on note cards and then quiz each other.

## Fabulous Fact

Earth has the perfect amount of gravity to have an atmosphere that is about 62 miles (100 km) thick, exactly right to shield the earth from the harmful rays of the sun and keep wild temperature swings from doing nasty things like evaporating all the water on the earth.

## Fabulous Fact

Water vapor makes up an average of about 1% of the gases in the atmosphere, but the amount it makes up where you are may be quite different from that. Some places have much more humidity (water in the air) than other places. Consider the difference in humidity between Phoenix, Arizona and Atlanta, Georgia.

Air and water are so common that people hardly notice their presence, but they are both vital for life, and they are also complex systems with complex chemical reactions happening within them and between them and living things.

Air is made up of many gases including oxygen, nitrogen, carbon dioxide, methane, ozone, argon, and many others in tiny amounts. Besides being necessary for respiration in living organisms, the air provides a cushion from the harshness of outer space and a shield from the sun and from objects colliding with the earth. Air is also essential for many chemical reactions that we take for granted, like the burning of fuel in our cars that allows us to drive.

Water is just as essential for life as air. We have never found a living thing able to survive without water. This is because water is so good at dissolving a wide variety of things and acts as an excellent vehicle to transport nutrients and waste. Water is so good at dissolving things that it is almost never pure. Water covers more than 70% of the surface of the globe and is the most plentiful of our natural resources.

## ☻ ☻ EXPLORATION: Composition of the Air

This diagram shows how much of each gas is in the air.

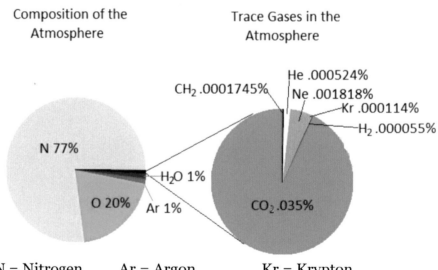

N = Nitrogen  Ar = Argon  Kr = Krypton
$CH_2$ = Methane  Ne = Neon  $H_2$ = Hydrogen
O = Oxygen  $H_2O$ = water vapor  $Co_2$ = Carbon Dioxide
He = Helium

At the end of this unit you will find a diagram to color. As you color it, talk about how some of these gases are essential for life on

Earth. Nitrogen is used in all living things, and plants must have it to survive. Certain microorganisms called "nitrogen fixing bacteria" take nitrogen from the air and put it into soil where plants can use it. Animals and people get nitrogen from the plants they eat.

Oxygen is used by animals and humans for respiration (breathing). Oxygen is also essential for burning, an important natural process and also one very useful to humans.

Water vapor is important in regulating the temperature of the earth. It is the most important of the greenhouse gases, keeping heat trapped near the earth instead of allowing it all to escape to space.

Carbon dioxide is another important greenhouse gas. It is also essential for plant respiration.

### ☺ ☺ ☺ EXPERIMENT: Air is Needed to Burn

Antoine Lavoisier discovered that oxygen is necessary for combustion, disproving the widely accepted theory of phlogiston. Alchemist J.J. Becher had come up with the theory that there must be a substance within things that burned in air, and he named that stuff phlogiston. It made sense, so everybody agreed it must be so.

When Lavoisier burned phosphorus it increased in weight. Lavoisier concluded it must therefore be gaining matter from the air since there was no other source possible. Further, it was noticed that in the absence of air, a candle flame would go out. He concluded that air was necessary for combustion.

Design an experiment to determine if air is required to burn a candle flame.

### ☺ ☺ ☺ EXPERIMENT: The Weight of Air

Air is real stuff, and it has weight. There are miles and miles worth of weight from the air pushing down on you all the time. The weight of air is called air pressure. You'd be crushed like tin foil in a trash compactor if you didn't have equal amounts of pressure inside your body pushing back against the air.

You can see this happen to a soda pop can if we remove the air pressure from the inside of the can.

1. Prepare a bowl of ice water and set it next to your stove.
2. Put a tablespoon of water inside an empty pop can.
3. Heat the can on the stove until steam begins to escape the can. Then heat for another minute.

## Fabulous Fact

Water is transparent in sunlight. You may not think that is significant until you realize that if it were not, water plants, which provide most of the oxygen for earth, could not live.

## Additional Layer

Look at a map of Earth and identify the largest cities on the planet. Almost all of them are located along rivers or coastlines of oceans. Why do people live near water? And why does water allow for and encourage greater population density?

## Additional Layer

The reason water is such a good solvent is because of its polarity (see the "Attractant" experiment from this unit). Water actually pulls apart the attractions within other substances and makes them cling to the water instead.

Oceans are full of dissolved chemicals, most of them natural. It's also easy to pollute water.

4. Using tongs, quickly invert the soda can into the ice water so the opening of the can is completely covered by the water.

The can should crush quickly and loudly. Heated air, as you produced in the can, is less dense, the molecules are moving faster than in unheated air. When you quickly cooled the air in the can by putting it in ice water and also prevented the can from getting more air inside it, you created a situation where there was less air pressure inside the can than outside. The heavy weight of the air pressing down on the can crushed it.

## ☺ ☻ EXPERIMENT: Universal Solvent

A solvent is a substance that dissolves other substances. Dissolving means to break apart into individual molecules. Water is a very good solvent and dissolves many things like salts, acids, sugars, alkalis and some gases, most importantly oxygen. All of these things that can dissolve in water are known as miscible. Things that do not dissolve in water, like fats and oils, are called immiscible. The ability of water to dissolve things is very important because it is water that carries nutrients and minerals around the planet, and it is water that carries nutrients and minerals and cell parts around living bodies. Water is needed by living things to form and break apart molecules chemically during metabolism. Also, the ability of water to dissolve oxygen is important to things that live in water, such as fish who can extract oxygen from water.

Gather a bunch of different household chemicals and substances, and predict whether they will dissolve in water. Here are some ideas of things you probably have lying around: salt, Epsom salts, pepper, candy coated sprinkles, flour, lemon juice, oil, vinegar, borax, soap, honey, sugar, cream, and butter. Raid your laundry closet and your kitchen cabinets for more ideas. Be careful though. Do not mix cleaning chemicals with each other, especially bleach and ammonia, which forms a deadly gas when mixed.

One more dissolved substance you can test out is oxygen. You can't see oxygen whether it is dissolved in water or not, so we'll observe it as it leaves the water quickly. This is called boiling. Pour some tap water into a saucepan and heat it on the stove. Watch as bubbles form on the bottom of the pan and float up through the water, bursting at the top. The bubbles are formed from oxygen gas which has been dissolved in the water. After water is boiled it has a "flat" taste. This is because the oxygen has been forced out. Vigorous shaking of the water will restore the good taste as oxygen is mixed back in. Try it.

### ☺ ☻ EXPERIMENT: Hard vs. Soft Water

Hard water is water that has minerals in it. The high mineral count is usually comprised of calcium, magnesium, and other minerals that are dissolved in the water. You can't usually see whether or not you have hard water just by looking at it, but you'll probably be able to tell other ways. One way people quickly notice is that they tend to get a "ring around the tub" and other mineral deposits in their sinks and bathtubs. You can also tell if you have hard water by how it lathers. Water with a lot of minerals won't bubble up as much when soap is added as soft water will. You can easily see the difference by comparing plain water with hard water that you mix yourself in this hard water experiment.

You'll need:
- 2 plastic cups
- a permanent marker
- 2 straws
- water (works best if this is soft water that you begin with – through a water softener or distilled water)
- plaster of Paris
- dish soap

## Additional Layer

Water's clinginess means it is attracted to the sides of containers, forming a bowl shape at the surface. This bowl shape is called a meniscus.

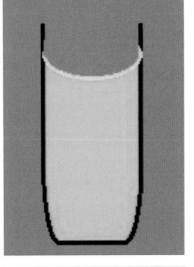

## Fabulous Facts

When stars are formed they create a rapidly expanding cloud of dust and gas which collides with the gases already in the space around the forming star. The collision of these gases makes hot shock waves which produce copious amounts of water vapor. Huge clouds of water vapor, much larger than earth's oceans, have been observed in space.

Here's an article from NASA talking about water clouds in space: http://www.nasa.gov/topics/universe/features/universe20110722.html

## Additional Layer

Most people prefer soft water for cleaning, but hard water for drinking. In the laundry, when doing dishes, when cleaning the bathroom, and even when cleaning ourselves, soft water is best.

It works well with soap and doesn't leave a nasty residue. However, most people prefer the taste of hard water.

Try to drink distilled water. You probably won't like it.

It's the minerals within water that make them taste good to us. A lot of people have favorite brands of bottled water for this reason. You might think, "It's just water. It's all the same." But that's actually not true. It's not the actual $H_2O$ flavor that we like in the bottled water; it's the minerals within it. Try doing a blind taste test of several brands of bottled water and see which you prefer.

1. Begin by labeling one cup "plain" and the other "hard." Put distilled water in each of the two cups.
2. Stir a spoonful of plaster of Paris (calcium sulfate) into the cup labeled "hard." It's not entirely soluble, but that's okay. By adding calcium to the water you are creating your own hard water to test.
3. Add a few drops of dish soap into each cup, and stir it in.
4. Now put a straw into each cup and begin gently blowing air into the water.

Both will bubble up somewhat, but the soft water will produce more bubbles.

Record the results of your experiment. Write about what you've learned about water in your science notebook.

## ☺ ☺ ☺ EXPERIMENT: Attractant

Water is a polar molecule. The oxygen retains a negative charge, and the hydrogens remain slightly positive. This is an important feature of water because it causes water to cling to itself and to other things. Water has a high surface tension, allowing water striders to skim along the surface and, most importantly, allowing water to cling to the sides of a small tube in what is called capillary action. This is so important, because it is how plants get water from their roots to their leaves, through the capillary action of water.

Try these experiments to show water's attractive quality.

### Drops Into Pools

Place a piece of waxed paper on your countertop. Use a dropper to put small drops of water on the wax paper. Observe the shape of the drop. Water beads up in little round drops instead of spreading and coating evenly. You can try dropping oil on the surface also to compare. Now get a toothpick and get it nicely wet. Bring it near one of the drops of water until it "jumps" and

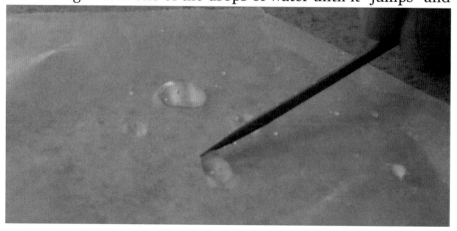

clings to your toothpick. If you move slowly and gently you can drag your little drop of water around the wax paper bit by bit and make the drops of water join together. You can keep adding your drops together to make one nice little pool.

## Over the Top

Fill a narrow tube, like a test tube, with water to the top. Then use a dropper to add in more water until the water level actually bulges above the top of the container. Water can bulge above because of its desire to cling to itself. Try the same thing with oil. Is oil a polar molecule?

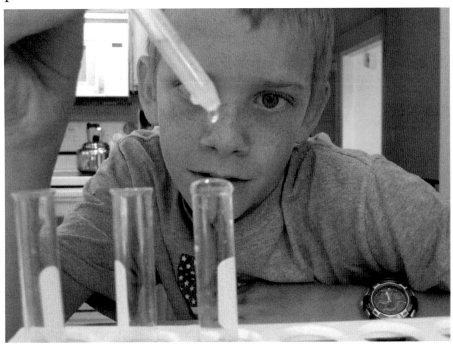

## Capillary Action

Fill one glass with water and have a second glass empty. Set the two glasses near one another on a countertop. Now take a paper towel and roll it into a tube. Place one end of the paper towel in

## On the Web

This video from Amoeba Sisters about "Properties of Water" is great for younger kids from about 8 to 13 years old.

https://www.youtube.com/watch?v=3jwAG-Wky98c

## Additional Layer

This is a poem by Ralph Waldo Emerson, an American poet and philosopher. It is about water and uses it as a metaphor for civilization.

### Water

*The water understands*
*Civilization well;*
*It wets my foot, but prettily,*
*It chills my life, but wittily,*
*It is not disconcerted,*
*It is not broken-hearted:*
*Well used, it decketh joy,*
*Adorneth, doubleth joy:*
*Ill used, it will destroy,*
*In perfect time and measure*
*With a face of golden pleasure*
*Elegantly destroy.*

Think about how water is beautiful, useful and necessary while also being one of the most destructive forces of nature. How is it being compared to civilization in this poem?

Take some time to talk it over and then memorize the poem and remember both the properties of water and how it can have two sides, like people.

the full glass and the other end in the empty glass. Then watch. The water will move along the paper towel and into the empty glass. This is how plants move water and the nutrients within it up their stems, from the roots that have lots of water to the leaves that have little water.

## ☺ ☺ EXPERIMENT: Freezing Water

Water freezes at 32°F (0°C). But if you dissolve a whole bunch of salt in the water, you can change the freezing point.

You need two cups of water, salt, a thermometer, and a freezer. Fill both cups about half full of water. Add table salt to one of the cups, about a tablespoon at a time, stirring as you go, until no more salt will dissolve in the water. Label the salty water cup with an S. Record the temperature of the water in each cup. Place them in the freezer of your fridge for thirty minutes and take the temperature of each cup again. Record. Continue recording the temperature of each cup every thirty minutes for the next four hours. Note when the water in the cups begins to freeze. Leave the cups in the freezer overnight and check them again the next day.

The salty water never freezes. Salt lowers the temperature that the water freezes at, and your refrigerator freezer never gets that cold. If you have a chest freezer, you can see if it gets cold enough to freeze saltwater.

It is important that salty water doesn't freeze as well as fresh because if it did, we would have frozen oceans, even in the tropics. Down deep the ocean is much colder than your freezer, even at the equator, and all that water would be frozen. Our whole planet would be a frozen, uninhabitable place.

## ☺ ☺ ☺ EXPERIMENT: Solid Water

As substances change from solid to liquid they become less dense. The molecules are able to slide over one another and move about more. This is true except in water. Water actually becomes more dense as a liquid than as a solid, the only known substance to have this property. This is important because it means that ice floats.

Every year the lakes and rivers where I live freeze over partially during the winter. If the ice formed on the bottom of the lake instead of on the top, it would stay frozen and build underwater icebergs that, insulated by the water above, would remain frozen throughout the year, making life in the water next to impossible. The oceans would all be frozen solid except perhaps a few dozen feet near the surface. Think about that.

Design an experiment that proves that water is more dense and takes up more volume when it is solid than when it is liquid.

## ☺ ☺ EXPERIMENT: Blue Vitriol

Water is often present in things that don't look remotely watery. For this experiment you'll need copper sulfate (from a science supplier) and a gas burner.

1. Place 1 tsp. copper sulfate into a heat-proof glass container.
2. Heat it over an open flame, like a Bunsen Burner or gas stove, until it turns white.
3. Remove it from the heat and allow the glass container to cool.
4. Squirt a bit of distilled water onto the copper sulfate crystals, and watch them turn blue again.

Copper sulfate contains water embedded and bound with the crystals. When it is heated the water evaporates off, and the crystals turn white. They turn blue again when you add water back in. The crystals, when returned to blue, are called Blue Vitriol.

For more fun, add even more distilled water, and stir to dissolve the crystals. Then pour them into a dish and set the dish in a sunny windowsill to evaporate. You will grow big, blue, beautiful crystals.

You can also take a part of the aqueous blue solution and add a bit of steel wool. The reaction that occurs is exothermic, producing heat. This is the reaction you're making happen. The copper is replaced with the iron, a process we learned about in Unit 3-19, Oxidation and Reduction.

$$Fe + CuSO_4 \longrightarrow FeSO_4 + Cu$$

### Famous Folks

Henry Cavendish was an English scientist who first discovered that water is made of hydrogen and oxygen, two gases.

Cavendish was also extremely shy, even foregoing to publish some of his brilliant findings. Read more about him.

### Writer's Workshop

Have your high schooler read through this article about water from HowStuffWorks.com, then write a short report about some of the properties of water.

http://science.howstuffworks.com/environmental/earth/geophysics/h2o.htm

# THE ARTS: WAR ART

## Memorization Station

Memorize the 3 Ps of War Art:

1. Propaganda

2. Patriotism

3. Protest

Watch for explanations of each in the unit and be able to explain what each P means.

## Deep Thoughts

There are other noteworthy tidbits in *The Death of General Wolfe*. Many believe that the Native American was inspired by Rousseau's Noble Savage concept, which presents the idea that uncivilized people are virtuous, not having been corrupted by civilization.

The men on the right are clasping their hands together, as if in prayer.

The man with the blue coat is Dr. Thomas Hinde. He tried to save General Wolfe and held him as he died.

Henry Brown is the lieuenant holding the British flag.

Why do you think all of these innocent, virtuous, and patriotic men were included in the scene?

Art often follows the story of the world. When there are times of prosperity and goodness, art reflects that. Likewise, in times of sadness, death, or despair, that mood is reflected in the art being produced. In times of war we tend to see art that is full of strong emotion. It is used to express the feeling of the time.

Art is also used to send messages and convince viewers to feel and believe certain things. For example, if I showed you a picture of all of the atrocities of war, you might feel a longing for peacetime. If I show you a picture of your country's great successes in the battle, you may feel pride and patriotism. And if I show you the horrors your enemy has brought to the world, you may feel a strong need to fight against that enemy.

War art has been used over the centuries to tell the stories of battles and nations, to help us feel the mood of the time, and to influence us to feel certain emotions.

This painting by Benjamin West is called *The Death of General Wolfe*. It depicts the 1775 Battle of Quebec during the Seven Years' War. General James Wolfe is the dying character at the center of the painting. This scene tells the story of the 15 minute long battle which was won by the British over the French at the cost of her general. Wolfe became a hero and a reason for the British to keep fighting.

We'll look at war art that spans many wars and many ages in this unit. As we do, watch for sadness, pride, patriotism, and persuasion.

☺ ☺ ☻ **EXPLORATION: Telling The Story of War**

If you aren't actually in battle, it's hard to know what it would be like. Artists tried to tell the story of war by depicting realistic scenes. This is a scene by William-Barnes Wollen called *Canadians at Ypres* from the trenches of World War I. Does the painting help you understand what it would have been like to be there?

Look closely at the painting; examine it. Choose one soldier and look at him especially closely. Imagine what he saw and heard and felt that day. Think of his story.

Now write a letter home to your family as if you are that soldier. Tell your family about what war is like and some of your experiences. Use the painting to tell the story of war.

☺ ☺ ☻ **EXPLORATION: Showing The Mood**

Even abstract art often felt harsher when it was depicting war. Umberto Boccioni made this futuristic style painting, *Charge of the Lancers*. It has sullen colors and harsh lines that speak of the sadness and hardness of war. Although abstract, it is a pic-

ture of a horse overcoming bayonets held by the Germans during World War I.

Use one of the paintings from this page as inspiration to make an abstract version of a painting of a battle scene. Remake the picture in your sketch-

**Additional Layer**

This painting called simply, *Tank*, was made by William Orpen using chalk, watercolor paints, and charcoal.

The evolution of technology is also shown in art. What are some new technologies invented in your lifetime that wouldn't have appeared in the art made previously?

**Additional Layer**

Souvenirs also became a hot commodity, beginning with the World Wars. Artists and artisans made handkerchiefs, decorated artillery shell casings, created ash trays made of bullets, and made other souvenirs for the soldiers to buy. Peddlers sold trinkets to the soldiers for themselves and to send home to their families.

## Additional Layer

Painted helmets were made for American soldiers by German Prisoners of War during World War I. The helmets had flags, maps, camouflage, symbols, and battle scenes painted on them.

## Writer's Workshop

Today many people call propaganda "fake news." It can be difficult to know what news is real and what isn't. All too often the people telling the news stories want to convince their viewers and readers of their own viewpoint, so they tell just part of the facts instead of telling both sides of a story. Very often the truth lies somewhere in the middle of the two sides telling the story.

What do you think you can do to determine the truth about issues? Write about the ways you will make up your mind about issues and what you can do to get reliable information, or at the very least, both sides of a story.

book so it no longer depicts a realistic scene, but shows an abstract version of that same event. What colors come to your mind when you think of a battle? What kinds of lines will you use to communicate the feeling of the painting you chose?

## ☺ ☺ ☺ EXPLORATION: The Poster

Posters became a new medium for artists during World War I, a trend that continued in World War II and beyond. Posters started popping up everywhere. They were advertisements, hoping to convince viewers to take sides.

Each country's posters depicted their own forces and symbols heroically. Make your own war poster on a piece of poster board. Use your country's colors and symbols and show the strength and heroics of your native land.

## ☺ ☺ EXPLORATION: Propaganda

Propaganda is information that is deliberately spread widely to help or harm a person, group, or nation. During wars, propaganda runs rampant. War posters were a common form of propaganda, but there were others as well. Fliers, stamps, newspapers, radio broadcasts, books, and films all supported the war efforts at home and villainized the enemy. No matter what country and what side of the conflict, there was propaganda to support it.

Look at these two similar, but opposing examples:

The first one is an Italian poster that shows the American Statue of Liberty depicted as a skull-faced angel of death. The words translate to, "Here are the Liberators," saying that Americans were killers, not liberators. Below the statue is an Italian city on fire after being bombed.

The second one is a forged stamp made by Americans. It shows Adolf Hitler with a skull-like face to equate him with death. It was patterned after an actual German stamp with Hitler's profile on it. The fake stamps were attached to letters and leaflets and airdropped all over Germany by Americans during World War II.

Use the Design-A-Postage Stamp printable from the printables page at Layers-of-Learning.com. You'll find it in the Geography Printables section. Make your own war stamp propaganda.

## ☺ ☺ ☺ EXPLORATION: Patriotism

Patriotism was a strong theme among a lot of war art. At the same time that enemies were depicted harshly, homelands were often depicted heroically. Countries wanted their citizens to be behind the war efforts. Many a battle has been won because of morale rather than merely strength or skill.

This oil painting made by Frederic Edwin Church shows wispy orange clouds over a deep blue, starry sky. If you look closely though, you'll see that the sky is actually a picture of the flag of the United States. This was painted during the U.S. Civil War as a statement about patriotism and love of country.

**On The Web**

Go to YouTube and watch The Power of Propaganda, a montage of television commercials that utilizes modern propaganda to sell us things.

https://youtu.be/ohoX-Z6EcneA

**On The Web**

Watch Top 10 Propaganda Posters by WatchMojo.com on YouTube.

https://youtu.be/m1HXDmQ9ZRs

The video shows ten propaganda posters with video clips and explanations about each poster to put it into context. This is most suitable for older kids as it shows wartime images and videos that may be frightening.

**Fabulous Facts**

The Office of War Information was created in the United States six months after the country entered World War I. The office's job was to create propaganda that would encourage Americans to get behind the war effort. They did this both by boosting the image of America and its allies and villianizing the enemy countries and forces.

## Additional Layer

Here are some more patriotic paintings. This is *George Washington Crossing the Delaware*.

This Japanese print is called *Secure the Homefront Defense*.

And this French painting is called *Bonaparte at the Bridge of Arcole*.

Make a watercolor painting of your country's flag in your sketchbook. If you can creatively set it in a scene, all the better.

### ☺ ☻ EXPLORATION: Protest

Protest art was also common during times of war. Many controversial wars, unpopular legislation, and dictatorial leaders have been a trigger for the creation of protest art.

Watch this video, Art of Protest, about what makes good protest art and take notes about the characteristics of a good persuasive protest sign as you watch. https://youtu.be/368siXUbO3A

Make your own protest sign about a cause you have learned about in history or one you currently feel strongly about. This could be anything from a current event on the news or just Mom's decision to make broccoli with dinner tonight.

### ☺ ☻ EXPLORATION: Front Lines

Being on the front lines was an ordeal for soldiers. Artists who painted war often painted the front lines because that was the place of greatest emotion and impact. Quite often the paintings of the front lines showcased the ragged exhaustion and shock of the soldiers who faced the harshness of war.

There was a phrase coined for the blank, unfocused look that soldiers got after being at war for awhile - the 2,000 yard stare. This painting is called *The 2,000 Yard Stare*. It is showing a man who has seen too much violence, known too much fear, and experienced too much trauma.

This soldier's stare is unforgettable. Practice sketching eyes in your sketchbook. If you'd like some help with the technique of drawing eyes, go watch the video, How To Draw A Realistic Eye: Narrated Step by Step by Circle Line Art School.

https://youtu.be/UL6QxeVl-RrQ

Use the eyes that you practice as the main feature while you show a soldier's 2,000 yard stare in your sketchbook.

## ☻ ☻ ☻ EXPLORATION: War Artists

Governments often hire official war artists to go into combat and record the experiences and stories of war. Some artists are there more coincidentally though, as soldiers who want to record their experiences. And others are just witnesses to the events or prisoners of war. Each of these would have a different perspective and perhaps show a different side of a war.

Divide a sheet of paper into thirds. In each one, draw a war scene from a different point of view - first, from a government hired war artist, second, from a painter who was drafted as a soldier, and third, from a prisoner of war who is captured in a cell.

*This is Kriegsmaler Frankreich, a German World War II artist in France in 1941. Photograph by Bundesarchiv Bild under CC license.*

### Writer's Workshop

Write a series of thought bubbles on a sheet of paper. Fill in thoughts you think the soldier with the 2,000 yard stare may have running through his mind.

Now imagine that you could put a person with that same stare in another shocking background situation. What are some other scenes that could inspire this look? Make some thought bubbles for those as well.

### Deep Thoughts

Photographs can capture a moment, but paintings can often capture a span of time and then condense it into one scene.

Which one do you think is a more accurate depiction?

### On The Web

Watch the video What is Propaganda on YouTube.

https://youtu.be/9ejT-foiu6yY

It examines the way propaganda is used today to influence us and skew our points of view.

## Additional Layer

Dada art was made as a reaction to World War I. Dadaists were unhappy with the violence that wartime had brought to the world and created nonsensical collages, constructions, and pictures to showcase the irrationality in the world. Sometimes they even found items and signed their name, or a nonsense name, on the item, calling it art. They were making the point that the sense had gone from the world. This urinal was signed under a nonsense name by Dada artist, Marcel Duchamp and called art.

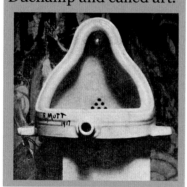

## On The Web

Watch The Story of Keep Calm and Carry On. This YouTube video by Barter-BooksLtd tells why the poster was made, how it was rediscovered, and how its popularity has since spread far and wide.

https://youtu.be/FrHk-KXFRbCI

## ☺ ☺ ☺ EXPLORATION: On the Home Front

Some war art didn't depict the fighting or the battles at all. There were plenty of people at home who were affected by wars being fought in distant lands. Even those who weren't directly fighting often made sacrifices and felt the pains of war. They too, needed to be convinced that their cause was just and that they were on the right side.

This painting by Norman Rockwell is called *Freedom From Want*. It's about one of Franklin Delano Roosevelt's Four Freedoms. It was published in newspapers with the a headline reading, "OURS. . . to Fight For. Freedom From Want." It is a statement about things that are worth fighting for, or in other words, things that are worth dying for.

Every time we engage in war we must ask ourselves what our purposes are. Is our cause noble? Is it worthy of the loss it will cause? Are we on the right side? Is it worth fighting for?

In the center of a sketchbook page write, "Things That Are Worth Fighting For." Surround the title by drawing pictures of things that you believe are worth defending. Include captions explaining your pictures.

## ☺ ☺ ☺ EXPLORATION: Keep Calm and Carry On Poster

As rumors of impending air raids leading up to World War II began, the British government produced a famous poster. Interestingly, at the time it wasn't very widely distributed and remained fairly obscure. The poster was rediscovered in 2000 and since then has become iconic British graphic art, being reproduced on everything from T-shirts to coffee mugs, not to mention pinned millions of times on Pinterest. Look online to see some adaptations of the poster. Make your own parody poster by filling in the blank in the phrase with something you like to do.

Keep Calm and _____.

For example, if you like to ride your bike, you might draw a bicycle icon and then write, "Keep Calm and Pedal On."

### ☺ ☺ ☺ EXPLORATION: The Kiss

At the end of World War II there was an iconic photo taken of a sailor kissing a nurse at the announcement that the devastating war was finally over. The two, strangers, were both standing in Times Square when the end of the war was announced. The sailor spun right around and kissed the nurse out of raw celebratory emotion. The photograph was published in Life Magazine.

Since that time the photo has been reproduced countless times. It is on postage stamps, post cards, and comic strips. Couples have imitated the pose for their own photos in Times Square. A sculptor named Seward Johnson even made a 25 foot tall version that stands in San Diego, California near the USS Midway, an aircraft carrier and maritime Museum.

Think about the war art you've looked at throughout this unit and write a narration that sums up the ways artists have captured war time and preserved its stories, emotions, and messages.

### Additional Layer

Read the Smithsonian Magazine article, Faces of War, about a group of artists who constructed masks for disfigured soldiers.

http://www.smithsonianmag.com/arts-culture/faces-of-war-145799854/

### Famous Folks

Matthew Brady was a famous photographer who captured the images of the American Civil War.

Coming up next . . .

Unit 4-12

Modern East Asia - the South

Food Chemistry

Modern Art

**My ideas for this unit:**

**Title:** _____ **Topic:** _____

_____
_____
_____
_____
_____
_____
_____
_____
_____
_____

**Title:** _____ **Topic:** _____

_____
_____
_____
_____
_____
_____
_____
_____
_____
_____
_____
_____

**Title:** _____ **Topic:** _____

_____
_____
_____
_____
_____
_____
_____
_____
_____
_____
_____

**Title:** _____ **Topic:** _____

_____

_____

_____

_____

_____

_____

_____

_____

_____

_____

**Title:** _____ **Topic:** _____

_____

_____

_____

_____

_____

_____

_____

_____

_____

_____

**Title:** _____ **Topic:** _____

_____

_____

_____

_____

_____

_____

_____

_____

_____

_____

# Battle of Britain

These are two fighter planes, one British and one German, fighting in the air over the south coast of England. Germany wants to invade Britain, but first they have to defeat the British planes. The British pilots were very young and very inexperienced, but very brave. They held out for four months against repeated air attacks by the Germans, saving Britain from a ground invasion and allowing the country to become the center of resistance to Hitler's plans for world domination.

# WWII Timeline

| April 1933 | June 1934 | 1935 | 1936 |
|---|---|---|---|
| The Reichstag burns; Hitler calls for emergency powers, new elections. Hitler elected president; abolishes all other political parties.  | Night of the Long Knives, Hitler has his opponents murdered  | Germany breaks the treaty of Versailles and begins to rearm; no one protests  | German forces occupy the demilitarized zone of the Rhineland, breaking the treaty again; no one protests |

| March 1938 | 1938 | Nov 1938 | March 1939 |
|---|---|---|---|
| Germany is invited to occupy Austria by the German Nazis who had seized power there; no one protests  | The Munich Agreement is signed, giving the Czech Sudetenland to Germany in an attempt to appease Hitler  | Kristallnacht, Nazis attack Jewish property all over Germany; 30,000 Jews are arrested  | Hitler seizes all of Czechoslovakia; no one protests  |

| Sept 1939 | April-May 1940 | May 1940 | July - Oct 1940 |
|---|---|---|---|
| Hitler invades Poland, meeting little resistance from the Poles; Britain and France declare war on Germany  | German troops invade Denmark, Norway, Belgium, the Netherlands, and France  | Miracle at Dunkirk; British troops evacuated  | Battle of Britain, the bombing of Britain by German planes, Britain holds out  |

| April 1941 | June 1941 | Dec 7, 1941 | April 1942 |
|---|---|---|---|
| Hitler occupies Greece and Yugoslavia. General Rommel is sent with his tanks to North Africa.  | Hitler launches a campaign against Russia to capture fuel supplies. They are defeated by the Russian winter. Russians join the Allies.  | Japan bombs Pearl Harbor, the U.S. declares war on Japan & Germany  | Japan occupies Burma, Hong Kong, Singapore, Malay, Indonesia, Thailand and the Philippines, plus the Chinese mainland and Korea which they occupied since the 1930s. |

| **May 4-8 1942** | **June 4-6 1942** | **7 Jan – 9 Apr 1942** | **August 1942** |
|---|---|---|---|
| Battle of the Coral Sea is a draw but halts plans to invade Australia  | Battle of Midway, U.S. decisively wins, Japanese advance is halted  | Battle of Bataan followed by the infamous Bataan Death March.  | Americans take Guadalcanal Island  |
| **November 1942** | **November 1942** | **1943** | **July 1943** |
| Allies win the Battle of El Alamein, securing North Africa.  | Russians win the Battle of Stalingrad  | Allies begin to bomb cities, both industrial and military targets in Germany  | Allies land in Sicily and begin to push the Axis out of Italy  |
| **June 6, 1944** | **September 1944** | **Dec 1944-Jan 1945** | **Feb 19 - Mar 26, 1945** |
| D-Day, Allies land at the beaches of Normandy, opening a western front  | U.S. begins liberation of the Philippines and Burma  | Battle of the Bulge won by Allies  | Americans take islands of Iwo Jima and Okinawa; positioned to bomb & invade Japan 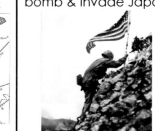 |
| **March 1945** | **May 7, 1945** | **August 6, 1945** | **August 14, 1945** |
| American and British troops reach German border and the Soviets enter Berlin  | Germany surrenders unconditionally  | Atomic bomb is dropped on Hiroshima, Japan killing 130,000; the Japanese remain defiant. 3 days later a second atomic bomb is dropped on Nagasaki killing 750,000  | Japan surrenders  |

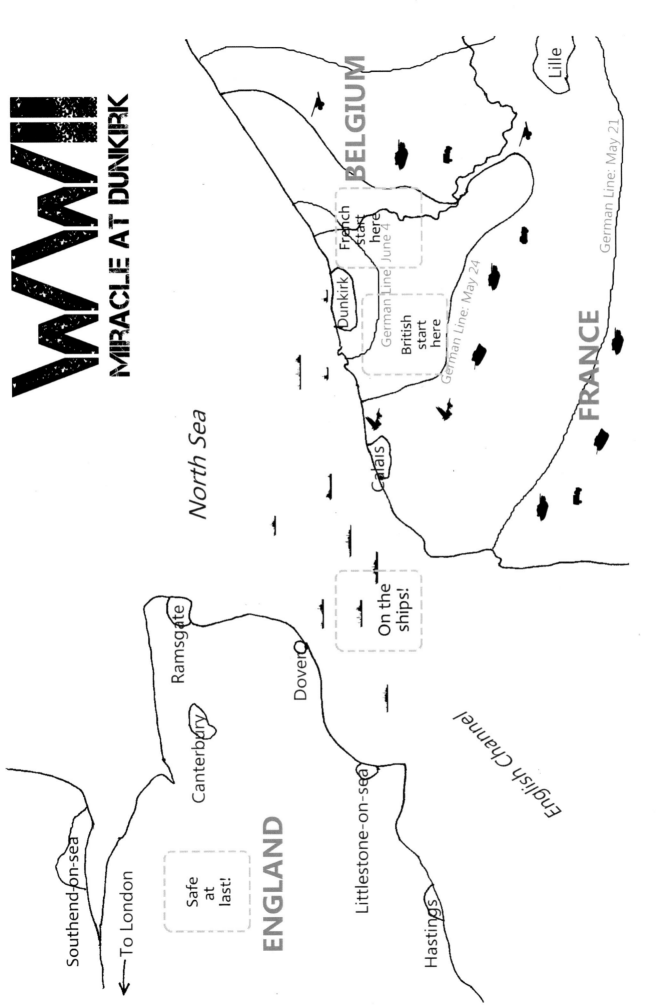

# WWII
## MIRACLE AT DUNKIRK

Save the soldiers who are trapped at Dunkirk! Roll 3 or more dice. For every odd die, lose a soldier card. For every even die, move a soldier card to the ships at sea. You'll have to get another even roll to get the soldiers safe to England.

| | | | | |
|---|---|---|---|---|
| 10,000 French Soldiers | 10,000 French Soldiers | 10,000 French Soldiers | 10,000 French Soldiers | 10,000 French Soldiers |
| 10,000 French Soldiers | 10,000 French Soldiers | 10,000 French Soldiers | 10,000 French Soldiers | 10,000 French Soldiers |
| 10,000 French Soldiers | 10,000 French Soldiers | 10,000 French Soldiers | 10,000 French Soldiers | 10,000 French Soldiers |
| 10,000 French Soldiers | 10,000 French Soldiers | 10,000 French Soldiers | 10,000 French Soldiers | 10,000 French Soldiers |
| 10,000 French Soldiers | 10,000 French Soldiers | 10,000 French Soldiers | 10,000 French Soldiers | 10,000 French Soldiers |
| 10,000 French Soldiers | 10,000 French Soldiers | 10,000 French Soldiers | 10,000 French Soldiers | 10,000 French Soldiers |

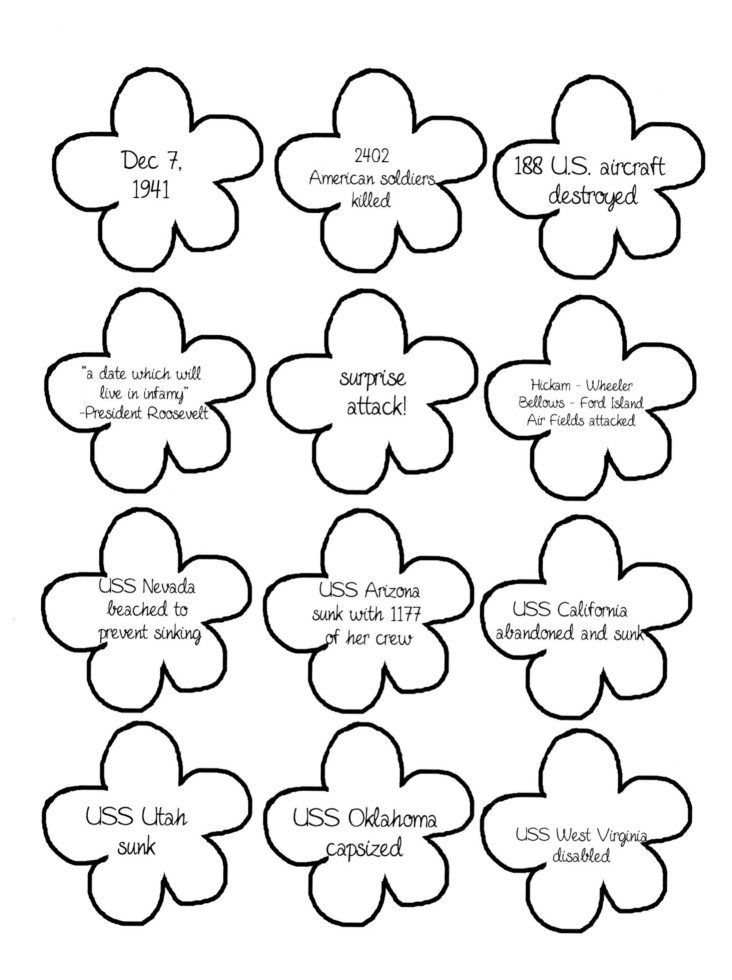

# INSTRUCTIONS

**1** This book is valuable. Do not lose it.

**2** Each stamp authorizes you to purchase rationed goods in the quantities and at the times designated by the Office of Price Administration. Without the stamps you will be unable to purchase those goods.

**3** Detailed instructions concerning the use of the book and the stamps will be issued. Watch for those instructions so that you will know how to use your book and stamps. Your Local War Price and Rationing Board can give you full information.

**4** Do not throw this book away when all of the stamps have been used, or when the time for their use has expired. You may be required to present this book when you apply for subsequent books.

Rationing is a vital part of your country's war effort. Any attempt to violate the rules is an effort to deny someone his share and will create hardship and help the enemy.

This book is your Government's assurance of your right to buy your fair share of certain goods made scarce by war. Price ceilings have also been established for your protection. Dealers must post these prices conspicuously. Don't pay more.

Give your whole support to rationing and thereby conserve our vital goods. Be guided by the rule:

*"If you don't need it, DON'T BUY IT."*

16—32299-1 ☆ U. S. GOVERNMENT PRINTING OFFICE : 1943

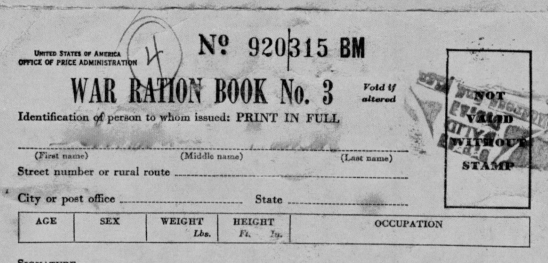

UNITED STATES OF AMERICA
OFFICE OF PRICE ADMINISTRATION

N⁰ 920315 BM

# WAR RATION BOOK No. 3

*Void if altered*

NOT VALID WITHOUT STAMP

Identification of person to whom issued: PRINT IN FULL

_____
(First name)　　　　(Middle name)　　　　(Last name)

Street number or rural route _____

City or post office _____ State _____

| AGE | SEX | WEIGHT Lbs. | HEIGHT Ft. In. | OCCUPATION |
|-----|-----|-------------|----------------|------------|
|     |     |             |                |            |

SIGNATURE _____
(Person to whom book is issued. If such person is unable to sign because of age or incapacity, another may sign in his behalf.)

**WARNING**
This book is the property of the United States Government. It is unlawful to sell it to any other person, or to use it or permit anyone else to use it, except to obtain rationed goods in accordance with regulations of the Office of Price Administration. Any person who finds a lost War Ration Book must return it to the War Price and Rationing Board which issued it. Persons who violate rationing regulations are subject to $10,000 fine or imprisonment, or both.

## LOCAL BOARD ACTION

Issued by _____
　　　　(Local board number)　　　　(Date)

Street address _____

City _____ State _____

_____
(Signature of issuing officer)

OPA Form No. R-130

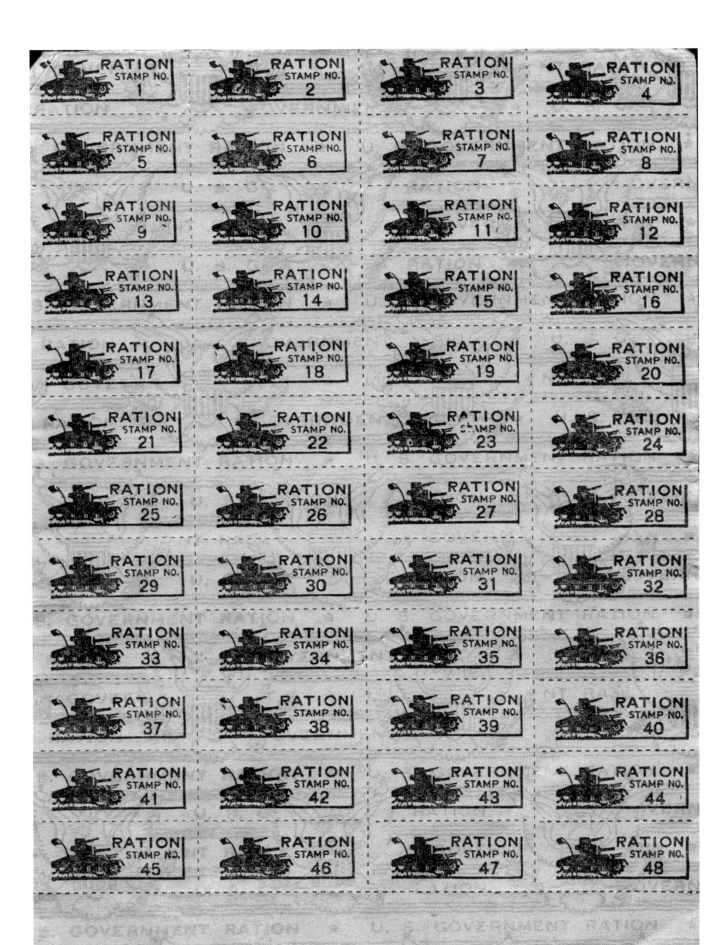

# Medals of WWII

## United States

**Medal of Honor**
Awarded for valor above and beyond the call of duty. The highest honor in the United States.

**Distinguished Service Cross**
Awarded for gallantry and risk of life in actual combat.

**Purple Heart**
Awarded to anyone who is injured or killed from enemy combat.

**WWII Victory Medal**
Awarded to those who served in the armed forces during WWII.

## United Kingdom

**Victoria Cross (VC)**
Britain's highest honor. Awarded for valor in the face of the enemy.

**War Medal**
Awarded to those who served in the military in WWII.

**George Cross**
Awarded for civilian gallantry in the face of the enemy. Created during the Blitz.

**Distinguished Service Order**
Awarded to higher ranking officers for meritorious or distinguished service during war time.

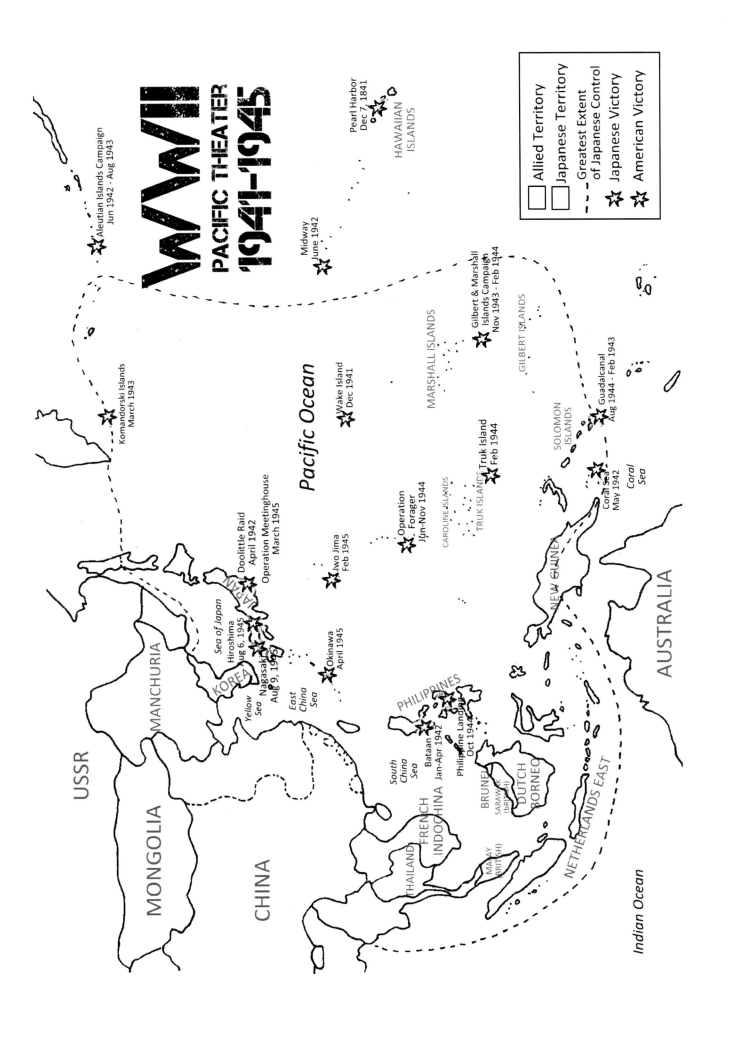

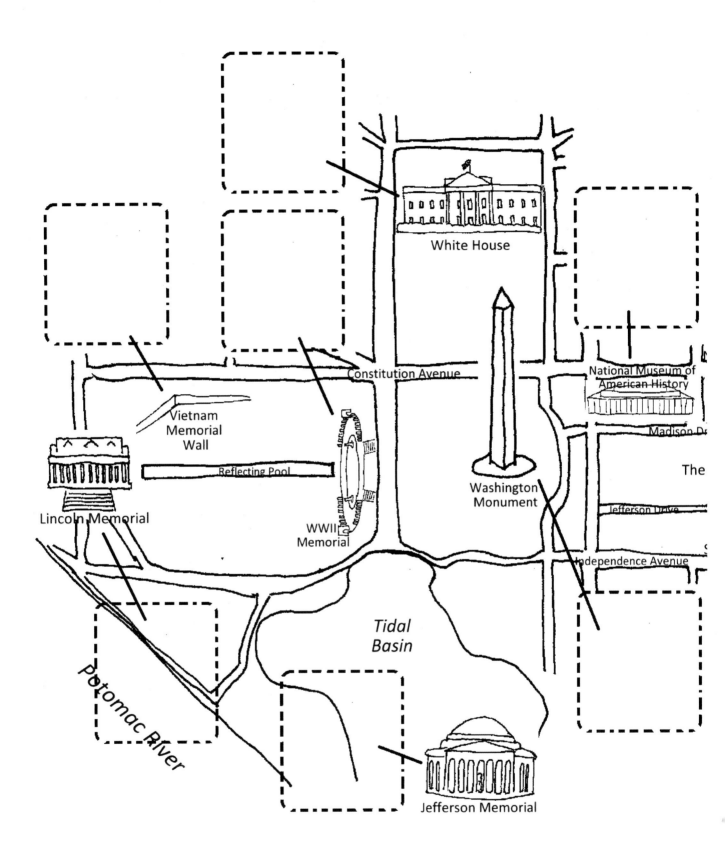

White House

Constitution Avenue

National Museum of
American History

Madison Dr

The

Vietnam
Memorial
Wall

Reflecting Pool

Washington
Monument

Jefferson Drive

WWII
Memorial

Lincoln Memorial

Independence Avenue

Tidal
Basin

Potomac River

Jefferson Memorial

# National Mall
## Washington, D.C.

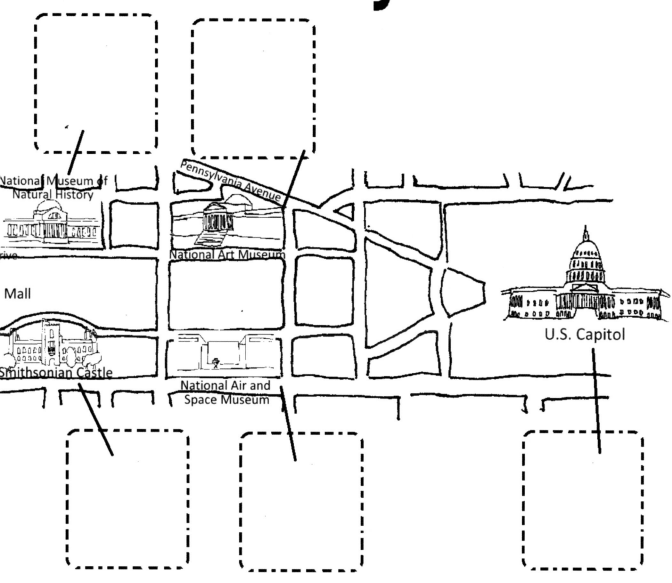

National Museum of
Natural History

Pennsylvania Avenue

National Art Museum

rive

Mall

Smithsonian Castle

National Air and
Space Museum

U.S. Capitol

# National Mall Cards

Read these cards and paste them to the map of the National Mall next to the buildings and memorials they describe. Color the National Mall as you go.

| | | | | |
|---|---|---|---|---|
| This fine art museum is free of charge. It was opened in 1937 and funded primarily by Andrew W. Mellon, a wealthy business tycoon. | Here you can see, free of charge, minerals, animals, fossils, plant specimens, and more. It is part of the Smithsonian Institution. | Collections include everything from Dorothy's ruby slipper to Little Golden Books. It's everything American at this stop on the Mall. | The largest collection of air and space craft in the world can be found here. This museum was established in 1946 when Truman was president. | Completed in 1852, this is the headquarters of the Smithsonian Institution. The building style is Gothic Revival and Romanesque. |
| This is the meeting place of the U.S. Congress. It was built in the Neoclassical style and first used in 1800. | This honors America's first president. Planned in 1848, it wasn't completed until 1884. When it was built it was the world's tallest structure. | This was built amid much controversy in honor of America's third president. The walls are adorned with quotes that supported the political agenda of our 32nd president. | Dedicated in 1922, this building honors the president who oversaw America's darkest hour, the Civil War. This is a popular place for historic speeches. | Constructed in 1982, this memorial honors military members who gave their lives for their country in the jungles of Southeast Asia. |
| Dedicated in 2004 to Americans who fought in WWII, this memorial consists of a pool and two fountains surrounded by 56 pillars and two triumphal arches. | Once known as "the Executive Mansion," this is where the president lives & works. It was completed in 1800, burned during the War of 1812, and rebuilt in 1817. | | | |

Draw in your own national heroes on the face of

# Mount Rushmore

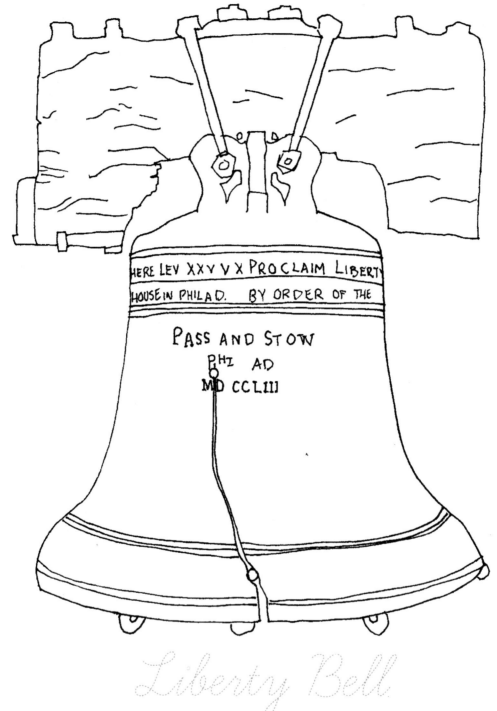

Liberty Bell

Proclaim liberty throughout all the land

unto all the inhabitants thereof

# Great Seal of the United States of America

Color the seal and then answer these questions about it.

1. How many arrows is the eagle clutching? _____

2. E Pluribus Unum means _____.

3. The olive branch in the eagle's talons represent _____ and
   the arrows represent_____.

4. The eye on the pyramid represents _____.

5. There is a pyramid on the reverse side of the seal to represent _____
   _____.

6. The date on the pyramid is written in Roman numerals, it means _____.

7. NOVUS ORDO SECLORUM means _____.

# Gases in the Atmosphere

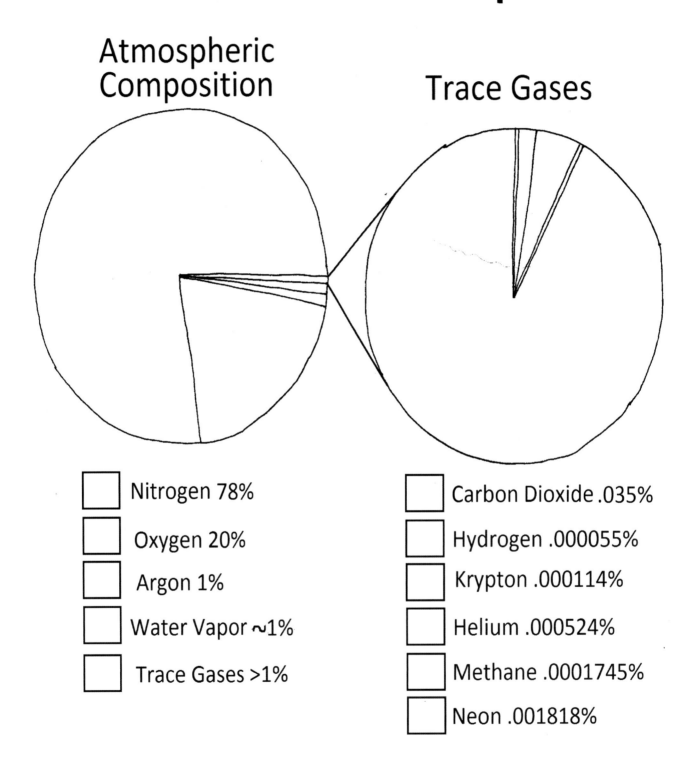

## Atmospheric Composition

## Trace Gases

- Nitrogen 78%
- Oxygen 20%
- Argon 1%
- Water Vapor ~1%
- Trace Gases >1%

- Carbon Dioxide .035%
- Hydrogen .000055%
- Krypton .000114%
- Helium .000524%
- Methane .0001745%
- Neon .001818%

# About the Authors

Karen & Michelle . . .
Mothers, sisters, teachers, women who are passionate
about educating kids.
We are dedicated to lifelong learning.

Karen, a mother of four, who has homeschooled her kids for more than eight years with her husband, Bob, has a bachelor's degree in child development with an emphasis in education. She lives in Idaho, gardens, teaches piano, and plays an excruciating number of board games with her kids. Karen is our resident arts expert and English guru {most necessary as Michelle regularly and carelessly mangles the English language and occasionally steps over the bounds of polite society}.

Michelle and her husband, Cameron, have homeschooled their six boys for more than a decade. Michelle earned a bachelors in biology, making her the resident science expert, though she is mocked by her friends for being the Botanist with the Black Thumb of Death. She also is the go-to for history and government. She believes in staying up late, hot chocolate, and a no whining policy. We both pitch in on geography, in case you were wondering.

Visit our constantly updated blog for tons of free ideas,
free printables, and more cool stuff for sale:
www.Layers-of-Learning.com

Made in the USA
Middletown, DE
04 April 2025

73769530R00040